HORSE SHOW BOYFRIEND

HORSE SHOW BOYFRIEND

My Crazy Year on
the Hunter/Jumper A-Circuit

By Austin Bell

Front Cover design by Austin Bell

Back Cover photos by Austin Bell, top to bottom:
WEF, Tryon, Kentucky, Miami, New Albany, Central Park, Upperville

For Meg

CONTENTS

Prologue

PART 1 - The Sport

PART 2 - The Shows

Epilogue

PROLOGUE

I am not your average Horse Show Boyfriend. I have nothing but respect for the semi-clueless beaus that are occasionally subjected to a few hours of watching their girlfriends guide horses over jumps, especially those exclusively limited to spectating hunter classes. You have my sympathy and you are my people. However, this book is not truly about me being one of you. If it were, it would read:

"I had to go to the show today for four hours to watch her ride for two minutes twice. It was extremely hot/cold and it smelled worse than her barn. Not really sure what happened. She got an ambiguously colored ribbon, and I made sure to get in the Instagram picture to have a permanent record of my attendance for when she undoubtedly forgets I was there in a few weeks. Hopefully, this is the last one I will have to go to for a month or so. The End."

Because of this experience, Horse Show Boyfriends are a pretty rare sight—much more so than the somewhat elusive Horse Show Dad and Horse Show Younger Brother. On the other end of the spectrum, you have the almost ubiquitous

Horse Show Mom, who might even go so far as to offer equitation commentary, attempt to handle tack or be your trainer.

I tell you this because I am technically a Horse Show Boyfriend, in that I am a boyfriend who is regularly at horse shows because of his girlfriend, but I am a very rare breed. For a time, I accompanied my girlfriend to horse shows not to watch her ride, but to help her as she covered them for her own horse show blog. I am one of the few males at a horse show with no link to anyone in the ring, no previous interest in the sport and no monetary reason to be there. I figured I needed to start writing about it, mostly because I needed to justify having to go to Pony Finals.

How did this all start? Let me take you back to the magical, long-ago time of January 2015. My girlfriend and I had recently moved back to her native South Florida from Los Angeles, where my career path had taken us after college. I spent time working in post-production on music videos. Everything would later come full circle when I would encounter equitation horses named after songs that had music videos I had worked on.[1] After three years in LA, my girlfriend was ready to move back closer to home, so we resettled in West Palm Beach when she landed a job there. I continued to work remotely for a company I was working for in LA, and six months passed by uneventfully as we avoided winter for yet another year.

---

[1] I can thank Don Stewart for this, a one-of-a-kind equitation trainer whose trademarks are naming his horses after pop songs and giving hilariously catty livestream commentary in a folksy drawl. One of my favorites of his is: "that round was going great for her, until she got to the first jump."

I had always known that my girlfriend was into horses. Her jumper she had competed on as a junior came to college with her and stayed at a nearby barn. She had stopped showing after high school and mainly just rode around for fun whenever she had time. Around the barn, I was relegated to chief carrot distributor. I mostly just tried not to look stupid in pictures with a horse she had known longer than me. I had no idea what was going on other than that it smelled at the barn and that it was funny that the bathrooms had very detailed signs about proper disposal of feminine hygiene products. After moving to LA, she briefly explored bringing him there before realizing the grim turnout options, opting instead to send him to a retirement ranch in Texas as he was almost 20 years old. Since then, her interest in horses manifested itself in the décor around the apartment—her saddle was in my home office, and we used a tack trunk as a coffee table. It wasn't until we moved to West Palm Beach that she expressed some excitement that we were very close to Wellington, a town where she had traveled from her home in Naples to compete while in high school. She mentioned that she was going to go check out the Winter Equestrian Festival (or WEF) when it started up in January. I joked that it would be great to have her out of the house and didn't give it a second thought. Suddenly it was January and one weekend she says, "I'm going to the horse show, can I borrow your camera?" I don't think she had ever used my low-end Nikon DSLR before, but I saw nothing wrong with it and gave her a few basic instructions before sending her on her way. She returned almost six hours later with a camera full of pictures, some of them turning out quite well due to her knowledge of the timing of jumping. After the first weekend, she decided to make a special Instagram account so as not to bombard her friends with horse show pictures, and she started finding the riders in the pictures to tag them. She couldn't stay away, going back every weekend for the duration of WEF[2] (I had not yet learned it went on for three months). She was quickly noticed for her ability to capture and caption the candid moments of the horse show world she loved. By the conclusion of WEF, she had over 15,000 followers and was very well-known around the intimate show community. She wanted to continue capturing shows after WEF ended. At my encouragement, she decided to quit her job to start a blog covering horse shows around the country. Since I can do my job remotely, I suddenly found myself co-piloting this rollercoaster in Horse Show World. That is how I came to be the rarest of Horse Show Boyfriends, the golden tiger of the schooling ring, if you will.

After a year, I felt these unique travels gave me a perspective on A-circuit hunter/jumper horse shows worth sharing, whether you've been showing since short stirrup or you have no idea what I just said and think it was just for alliteration. Before I went to WEF in 2015, my knowledge of the sport was mostly that it was, in fact, different than what they do at the Kentucky Derby (a big step for most). By virtue of being this rare breed of Horse Show Boyfriend, I have acquired enough horse show knowledge to be dangerous. I can now at least pretend to discuss a triple combination being far too forward before wondering how judge 2 could have possibly scored the Medal test an 82 after that missed lead change (clearly it was her BNT). I feel it is my duty to impart

---

[2] WEF is also the acronym for the World Economic Forum, which takes place every January in Davos, Switzerland. This makes for some confusing crossovers in social media hashtags during the weeks they overlap.

what I have learned and observed onto the unknowing masses while also giving the veterans of the sport a fresh perspective on something that has become second nature to them. If just one Horse Show Dad or Mom reads my book and refrains from congratulating their daughter after her 51 hunter round, I've done my job.

PART 1

The Sport

CHAPTER ONE

The Basics
Horses Jump Over Fences

Before I take you on my whirlwind journey across a bevy of A-circuit horse shows, I want to provide a brief overview of some of the overarching topics of the show world, starting with the basics. I promise it will be painlessly informative and not totally redundant for those of you who constantly have to explain to your friends that you aren't a jockey. Which brings me to my first point: show jumping is not horse racing. You could make the case that horse racing has more in common with NASCAR than it does with show jumping. Racing and jumping are both people riding horses... and that's where the similarities end. There are a few crossovers in the community, but they are mostly separate sports. Because of the general public's awareness of racing, the equine knowledge-challenged among us will generally assume that their show jumping friend's dream is to one day compete in the Kentucky Derby. The correct big event to strive for is the Olympics, where equestrian events (not racing) have been held at the summer games since 1900. The Olympics holds three equestrian events: show jumping, eventing, and dressage.

Dressage, which you are probably tangentially familiar with as the butt of some joke, is wildly different and involves no jumping whatsoever. People have called it a sort of horse ballet. To me and even to some show jumpers, it is beyond comprehension. Eventing is more of a triathlon which combines dressage and show jumping with a type of cross-country jumping where riders traverse open fields and jump enormous solid objects. It is abjectly terrifying, and I would need extremely strong medication in order to spectate my child participating in it. There is also another side of riding competition that uses a Western saddle as opposed to the English, or hunt seat saddle used in these disciplines—that is a completely different can of worms featuring barrels, ropes and cowboy hats.[3]

So we've established what doesn't happen at a hunter/jumper horse show: racing, cowboys or dancing, so, what does? Intrinsically, it involves a horse going over jumps in a ring (also called fences). This is the most comfortable comprehension level for those who attend a show to watch a loved one. Extra facts and terms may seep in, but when explaining it to someone else, it boils down to "yeah, she's really into the horse jumping thing." The first step towards greater understanding is determining the type of jumping discipline you are watching at a hunter/jumper show: hunter, jumper, or equitation. The main difference between these three disciplines is their scoring: jumper by speed and accuracy around the course, hunter by a subjective judging of the horse, and equitation by a subjective judging of the rider.

---

[3] In addition to jumping and dressage, English-type saddles are used in racing and polo. I learned the difference between the two saddles early on in our relationship when I pointed out everything horse-related to my girlfriend and more than often she would scoff and say "that's Western."

There are quite a few other things that separate them, but the main thing you need to know is time, horse, rider—everything else is mostly a variation from this basic distinction. They are different enough that most horses only compete in one of the disciplines, meaning you need multiple horses if you want to do more than one. My understanding and appreciation for each of the disciplines will be examined in their own chapters, but knowing of the existence of these three instantly upgrades you to a higher plane of understanding. When your new neighbor's kid mentions that she jumps horses, you can now respond with gusto, "Oh, hunter, jumper or equitation?" before having absolutely nothing else to add to the conversation.

Hunter/jumper shows have three distinct subgroups of competitors: juniors, amateurs and professionals. Juniors are riders under 18, amateurs and professionals are riders 18 and over who elect either to not make or make money in specific ways through the sport. A crash course in horse show lingo: classes are the specific events that riders compete in throughout the day, entries are the horse and rider pairings that compete in classes, and rings are both the physical location and discipline of competition (e.g., the hunter ring). Horse shows themselves are multi-day events that start as early as mid-week and go until Sunday. Top shows are classified by their difficulty and designated as "A-rated" shows, thus the grouping of these shows known as the "A-circuit." There is a decent chance that your coworker's friend who rides does local shows that are "B" or "C" rated and are a far cry from the subject matter of this book. Unless of course, you work at a hedge fund and your coworker is a millionaire. While there are small periods of downtime, there are horse shows basically year-round. Geographically, it is most popular in the northeast and Florida, and most of the shows I attended were on the east coast. Internationally, Western Europe joins the US and Canada as the major hotbeds of the sport, with smatterings elsewhere. I will discuss more on the vagaries of professional and international competition in their own separate chapters.

Another level of horse show comprehension is learning the lingo of the show and the horse. Specifically, the horse gear, or "tack" is chock full of very specific words that will have little meaning to those of you with no equine experience. I still confuse a halter and a bridle, which I refuse to clarify for myself on purpose so that I can at least in some way avoid transforming into a full-fledged horse person. It is not as important that you learn the minutiae of the horse world's vocabulary—just that you are curious enough while experiencing a horse show to pick it up naturally.

A final basic debrief on the types of horses: at shows, there are regular, full-sized horses, then there are ponies, which are smaller fully-grown horses. Ponies are not baby horses—these are called foals, and they are much cuter than ponies. Ponies are generally for younger children to ride because of their size before they graduate to horses. You will not see adults riding ponies at a show unless you are taking some of the good drugs. Horses of both genders are ridden at a show: mares are females, and both geldings and stallions are males. Stallions are not-castrated and are seen in the show ring—juniors are not allowed to show them. Most horses are between the ages of 5 and 20. Show horses also have specific breeds, almost all of which come from Europe and have names like Zangersheide, Dutch Warmblood and Holsteiner. The breed is not overly noticeable in appearance or performance and is only worth knowing because most Grand Prix events make a point of mentioning it when introducing the horse and rider. Show horses are for the most part "warmbloods," a mix of cold-blooded, calm and strong draft horses that are commonly used to pull things and hot-blooded thoroughbreds, which race.[4]

One of the easiest ways to ingratiate yourself is to accurately discuss the coloring of the horse, so you don't sound like a noob when you say, "I like that brown one over there."[5] Most show jumping horses are one of the following three: bay (brown-coated with black colored mane and tail), chestnut (brown-coated with brown colored mane and tail) or grey, which covers the spectrum of white and grey colored horses.[6] You will occasionally see a black horse, which is shockingly black with black mane and tail, or a pinto horse, which is black or brown with large white spots. Ponies have none of the breed distinctions and come in a host of other exciting colors like palomino (gold coat, white mane and tail), buckskin (gold coat, black mane and tail) and red roan (mixed white and bay coat, dark mane and tail). I'm still waiting to see a rainbow pony a la "My Little Pony" – those have to be real, right? Again, this is just a tasting of the plethora of general horse and horse gear and terms that will make the difference between your being able to communicate with horsey people instead of assuming they are jockeys.

---

[4] The exception to this rule are Off-the-Track Thoroughbreds, or OTTBs, which are acquired at usually a much lower price than warmbloods and re-engineered to compete in the jumping ring. OTTBs are not common at A-Circuit shows.

[5] After having many older family members question me about its meaning, I should mention "noob" is computer slang for "someone who knows little about something and shows little willingness to learn more."

[6] Junior riders have enthusiastically embraced the homophonic possibilities of the now-popular acronym "bae" and "bay."

Riding is a sport with all these terms and divisions, but above all, it is a lifestyle. If you ride on the A-circuit, you are automatically a part of a small but idiosyncratic community who spend a great deal of time and money on the sport. It's glamorous, fascinating and depressing all in one, with the competition sometimes seeming secondary to the real sport of VIP table mingling and travel. Hopefully, after reading this you will have at least a marginal grasp on not only the sport, but the culture that envelops it. But for now, let's move on to the competition and, most importantly, how to win.

CHAPTER TWO

Jumpers

What Your Friends Think Is Horse Racing

At a hunter/jumper show, the main form of competition is in the jumper discipline. The only confusion comes from the name: all of the disciplines involve jumping to some degree, but this one is referred to as the "jumpers," with hunters and equitation being less popular offshoots. I am eternally grateful the jumper discipline is what is held internationally and at big events like the Olympics, as it is the easiest to follow. Winning is determined by two things: rails knocked down and what was their time around the course. The main obstacle in the jumper discipline is a rail (and a lack of money). Any number of small errors can cause one of the horse's legs to collide with a rail mid-air and send it toppling over, giving you four jumping faults for your effort and shattering your chances of winning. You also can't take your time being careful, as the course designer sets a time allowed that you must complete the course in before you begin to accrue time faults—one for each second over in most cases. It's easy to figure both out, because one involves reading a clock and the other involves watching large wooden beams physically fall off jumps. All good scoreboards will even update as rails are knocked down and time faults are accrued, so you have very little excuse for not being able to follow a jumper class.

Most jumper classes begin with a first round, in which riders attempt to complete the course without any time or jumping faults, also called going clear.[7] If multiple riders go clear, then they will return for a second jump-off round. This takes place on an abbreviated version of the first round course. You will usually not see riders going extremely fast or taking chances until the jump-off, as it is more important in the first round to be careful and not knock any rails down. The winner in the jump-off is the rider with the fewest faults and fastest time. The elusive double clear is attained when riders manage to attain no faults in either round, giving them a chance to win the class if they have the fastest time of all the double clears. For smaller classes, riders will usually complete their jump-off course immediately after their first round. At the big events, though, riders will complete their jump-offs after all riders have finished the first round. Because none of the riders compete simultaneously, there are often riders with multiple entries (horses) in the same event to increase their chances of winning.

There are two competitive aspects of jumping that I particularly enjoy as a spectator. There is a lot of tension and build-up as riders go around a course attempting a clear round. As they approach the finish with a chance to move on to the jump-off, it becomes very exciting. Any decent crowd will applaud wildly when riders go clear in a Grand Prix or

---

[7] Not to be confused with the Scientology phrase. Though there are probably societal similarities.

groan when a rail comes down. To better follow this, you will need to know which jump is the last (it will have little timers on tripods after it) so you know when to start cheering if a rider does go clear. I also appreciate that in the jumping discipline, you don't need your round to be pretty, you just need to get around in time and go clear. It doesn't matter if you have the eq of a caveman, you rub more rails than a stripper and you have more chips than Famous Amos.[8]

The jumper discipline is the main competition division of show jumping because it has the most prize money and is what is done at the highest levels of professional competition such as the Olympics or World Equestrian Games. There are much fewer professional hunter riders and no professional equitation riders. One of the unique things about the sport is how variable its results can be because of the multitude of different factors involved: the type of course, the horse's mood that day and luck, to name a few. Top riders win frequently, but it is very difficult to pick a winner in a field at a Grand Prix because there are so many different aspects to winning and one small mistake can knock a rail down and put you out of contention.

The difficulty of a jumper division is determined by the maximum height of the rails of the jumps. The lower the height, the easier the class. The heights are measured in meters, with the lower-end classes ranging from 0.80 to 1.10 meters, or 2'9" to 3'7" high to the higher end around 1.50m or 5' high. An important note when discussing jump heights: you refer to them as "meter fifty" or "meter ten" and always

---

[8] To explain this: your "eq" refers to your equitation, or form while riding, rubbing a rail means touching it without knocking it over, and chips are results of taking off at an incorrect distance.

include a second decimal place. I learned this the hard way after saying "one point five meter classes" and writing "1.5m" numerous times, much to the embarrassment of my girlfriend. Some of the higher classes will have more difficult aspects to navigate like multiple jumps one after the other (called a combination), a pool of open water, or burning rings of fire.[9] Water is a formidable obstacle because it can cause horses to spook, or frighten in a way that makes it more difficult for them to go over a jump. Horses need to be well trained in order to avoid this instinctual hydrophobia. I am a little surprised that in all the years of show jumping there has not been more development of creative obstacles to spook horses than little plastic pools filled with water, elegantly referred to as liverpools.

The jumper course is filled with decorative jumps that usually display a sponsor logo and colors on the boards that hold the rails up, which are also called standards. A fun exercise is to see how well sponsored an event is according to how many of the jumps on a course are generic and how many feature a brand. There also is a level of creativity involved in crafting these jumps. I've seen: a saddle company sponsored jump with their actual saddles in plastic bubbles on the side of the jumps; the side of jumps just being large riding gloves; and even large pictures of ice cream or cookies. Even the non-sponsored jump designs can get crazy. At WEF, one of the first jumps I noticed featured 5-card poker hands on either side. Some featured the standard royal flush, a few with a straight flush, but some just had inexplicable full houses. I have some questions for whoever makes the decisions on which poker

---

[9] Just kidding about the rings of fire. Though some horses may actually think open water jumps are rings of fire.

hands they render into immortality via wood, and how exactly this relates to horses jumping. I also noticed exciting jumps like models of the famous Breakers Hotel in Palm Beach and iconic colored jumps featuring horse world brands like Hermes and Rolex. My favorite, however, was completely absurd: on either side it featured a heron playing a cello, and it was for a South Florida classical music station. Again I have no idea who thought of this, but I want whatever they were taking.

In all events riders must wear a show jacket, shirt with collar and breeches of some sort. In contrast to the hunter and equitation rings, jumpers can have blinged-out helmets, fancy bonnets that cover the horse's ears, saddle pads with logos, Swarovski crystals on their gloves—you name it, it appears in the ring. As long as you follow the basic tenets of the rules, you won't get kicked out of the ring. I'm still waiting for someone to really go all out with the wardrobe. Beating someone in a jumper division is one thing, but doing it while wearing a lime green show jacket with tassels really makes that blue ribbon special.

Many things can go wrong during a jumping competition. Sometimes, a horse will unexpectedly stop in front of a jump instead of going over it. This is called a refusal and counts for four jumping faults as if they knocked a rail down. Riders must circle back around and attempt to go over the jump again. If a rider's horse refuses twice in a round, they are eliminated. Another way to be eliminated is to go off-course, or go over the jumps in the incorrect order. Also, when riders fall off a horse, they are automatically eliminated. This turn of events is referred to as an unfortunate dismount and riders, if they are not severely injured, must then do a walk of shame with their horse back to the entrance while the announcer coaxes the crowd to applaud their failure and subsequent survival. Even grizzled veterans who have been riding horses since they could walk hold their breath when a fellow rider begins to fall, as the uncertainty that follows is truly terrifying. Most riders catch themselves easily, but there is always the chance of something much worse happening, reminding you why you have to wear a helmet when you ride. On the less dark side of things, riders sometimes will just up and quit in the middle of the round. If things aren't going their way—they've knocked a few rails down and have no chance at placing high enough to win prize money, riders in higher divisions will sometimes end a course early by doing a voluntary withdrawal or VW, to do what the announcers like to call "saving their horse for another day." Some days I feel like I need to do a voluntary withdrawal on myself and be saved for another day.

The design of the courses that the horses must complete is an alchemy all its own with professionals who specifically map out where jumps go for specific classes. This becomes very technical at the high levels, and the fond phrase for the art of course design is that the rider and horse pairings must "answer the questions the course asks of it." When I first heard this I laughed, but now I say it haughtily like everyone else in the hunter/jumper world. This phrase comes up frequently in press conferences when the winners are asked about the course and amusingly voice their approval. Of course they liked it, they just won.[10] I should also mention at this point that riders engage in a pre-competition ritual of

---

[10] The top two culprits some professionals blame their poor performance on instead of themselves tend to be course designers and the ring footing.

walking the course to learn it before showing. There is nothing notably interesting or funny about this except perhaps that they all mill around in straight lines or that I am usually the one fearfully holding my girlfriend's horse as she does it.

Quirks aside, the jumper division is the closest thing you might find to an actual spectator sport you can follow in the horse show world. After watching for a brief period of time, you can pick up most of the nuances and be an able participant in the fun. Before long you will be whispering uninhibited swear words while watching long spots like a veteran. Don't get used to it though—the rest of the crazy world of show jumping makes far less sense. You have about as much chance of being able to fully follow these other events as you do going in the ring and competing in them. But, the goal here is to be able to feign knowledge as a Horse Show Boyfriend, Dad, Mom, etc., so join me as we leave the exciting jumper world and go on a journey to the land of subjective scoring and pageantry.

CHAPTER THREE

Hunters
Not a Fox in Sight

Before the deep dive into the rabbit, or in this case fox, hole that is the hunter discipline, I warn you right away to abandon all logic. In my attempts to figure out the many "why" questions behind the hunter class, I was repeatedly met with the old adage "because that's the way it's always been done." At first to an outsider, very little of hunter competition makes sense. In a Zen sort of way, once you understand that hunters are not meant to be understood, then you can start to truly understand them.

As with other show jumping disciplines, hunter classes involve riding a horse around and over a course full of jumps, but that's where the similarities end. The basic distinction of the hunter discipline is that scoring is done subjectively, by a judge, on the horse's form going around the course, instead of an objective measure of time and jumping faults. The score is numerical and arbitrary, on a scale of 0 to 100. There is no set number of points added or subtracted quantitatively for anything done during a round.[11] A judge simply gives you a score of 84 because it feels like an 84 round to him or her. To say that this can be troublesome is barely scratching the surface of the dangers of imprecise, subjective scoring. It becomes difficult for a judge not to consider things like the reputation of the rider, trainer, or even horse when doling out scores. An entire book could be written on the politics of the hunter class which I am not remotely qualified to write. Scoring can vary drastically depending on the venue and judge, but most successful or winning rounds will score between an 80 and a 90 depending on the overzealousness of the judge, and anything below 60 can be seen as nothing short of a catastrophe. You will very rarely see anything above a 90, and only once in my travels did I hear of a 100 score.[12] Some classes will mercifully announce the score after the round to give you some idea of how the rider did, but just as many leave you guessing.

At its core, the hunter competition is much more of a beauty pageant with ancillary jumping activity. The main goal is to look pretty while navigating the course. This can be more difficult than it sounds, as distances between jumps must be perfectly assessed while managing the horses' wavering moods and actions. Where in the jumper ring a winning, double clear round can be riddled with miscues, any small mistake can derail a hunter's chances of victory. I admit that I have some biases against hunters because they are far less enjoyable to watch than jumpers for a less knowledgeable spectator. The combination of the very nuanced elements of

---

[11] One exception is in some competitions riders can earn a bonus point if they choose the higher of two jumps side by side on the course, or the high option. I knew some people in college who frequently took the high option.

[12] Tori Colvin. Who else?

the ride that are judged and the rounds' repetitive and languourous pace makes it very difficult to follow for someone new to the sport. Forgive me if I am less enamored of hunters as I go into more detail about them. I just haven't had a chance to appreciate their tradition or learn exactly what a swap off a lead change looks like.

In contrast to the jumper ring, dress code is strict—a rider must have very few extra accessories on his or her tack, and their horse's mane must be braided. The hunter course can best be explained by attempting to understand that the discipline's roots lie in fox hunting, where the primary purpose of riding a horse was to go out in the woods wearing red coats while hunting foxes.[13] It was a different time, before you could just order fox pelts in bulk on Amazon from your iPhone as you waited for the jog to be called. In an attempt to either fool the horse or cultivate some link to the past, the jumps on a hunter course are designed to be natural, that is, wooden with green and brown hues that slightly resemble trees or brush. There are no sponsored jumps in the ring, but hunter jumps do vary from basic faux-birch to large hay bales and stacks of wood. An important skill to have for any non-horse person is the ability to look in a ring and determine whether or not a hunter or jumper competition is going on—looking at the type of jumps is the easiest way to do this.

---

[13] There are many amusingly quirky aspects to fox hunting, but one of my favorites is that in order to wear a red coat on a hunt you must "earn your colors." I read more about this in Introduction to Foxhunting, which included such gems as "To be awarded colors means you are a member of the hunt who has met all the hunt's standards for hunting" and "The criteria to earn colors differs" but "most importantly anyone awarded colors should not be an embarrassment to their hunt should they hunt with another hunt." All this made me think twice about picking up a red show jacket for fun at the consignment store.

A hunter class's difficulty is less easy to discern than the jumper division—there are only a few different heights of jumps, 3', 3'3" and 3'6" being the main ones. Instead, hunter classes are divided by the rider's age and, at the junior and pony level, the size of the horse. For kids, pony hunter classes are the big events. Kids doing the pony hunters usually don't end up there by accident—there is generally some equestrian interest in the family that pushes them into doing it. From there, riders under 18 are separated by the children's and junior divisions, the latter of which has higher jumps. Upon turning 18, you graduate to the amateur owner division, with a select few riders opting to become professional. The main reason to become a professional is so that you can compete while riding other owners' horses. However, few amateurs do this, as they are usually able to afford their own horses for high level competition. The equivalent of the jumper Grand Prix is the Hunter Derby. Aside from reminding me of the name of a fraternity bro I knew in college, a Hunter Derby has a slightly modified format and features the female riders wearing specialized coats called shadbellies, which are essentially just coats with tails. For some reason, men don't get to wear these—they just have to sport a monocle (I wish). If you're wondering why this is—I have received no straight answers other than "that's just how they do it in hunters." Oh, okay.[14]

---

[14] I did research and the only definitive answer is that, in the USEF rulebook, shadbellies are not considered "formal hunt attire" for men. Further confusing matters is that in dressage, both men and women wear shadbellies. Either way, it seems silly to me that guys that do hunters don't have to buy an extra show coat. If I had a daughter, I would protest this and have her not ever wear a shadbelly.

The hunter horses, courses and competitions are very much unique to their discipline. Hunter horses, or just "hunters" as they are commonly called, mostly compete in only hunter classes because they are designed to look good going over jumps—not necessarily to be fast or jump high. This leads many riders to joke that their hunters are the "fat ones" compared to their svelte jumpers. A phenomenon I discovered early in my horse show journey was riders referring to their horses as "nuggets," a term of endearment meant to also imply they resemble the fast food chicken staple. Hunters are especially susceptible to being labeled as nuggets in conversation or on social media by their owners due to their larger physique. You may also hear riders referring to their horses as other animals altogether, such as giraffes, donkeys, or rabbits. You will almost certainly hear full-grown horses being referred to endearingly and incorrectly as "ponies." It seems like they are trying to confuse people like me who are attempting to learn about these things. If jumpers are the Ferraris, hunters are the Rolls Royces—smooth to ride and stylishly built. Despite the fact that there is less of a competitive arena for these horses in terms of prize money, hunters will fetch very high sale prices.

I also should add this brief interlude on hunter horses and the division: illegal drugging is arguably more prevalent. This is largely a result of judges generally looking for a quiet horse—that is, one that performs without incident or abundant outward energy. However, this is essentially asking most horses to be robotic and perform without any sign of their personality. As a result, there is immense pressure for riders to find ways to make their horses appear quieter than they might actually be to impress the judges. One way to do this is to tire them out with exercise before a competition and another is to give them illegal drugs that calm them down. There is some debate about which is worse for them, but both seem to be done more often than appropriate. There are many unexplored questions beyond my comprehension about the tension between the expectations for success as dictated by the judges in the hunter ring in contrast to the natural instincts of most horses.

Unlike the jumpers, hunter competition has many different elements of competition. It includes the similar main round, where a rider goes around a set course, sometimes called over fences. However, in contrast to a winding jumper course that tests speed, a hunter course is a leisurely stroll alternating between jumps around the perimeter and across the interior of the course. In most hunter classes, they do two of these rounds and score and award ribbons per class individually. I don't know why they do two rounds while a jumper only does one. I guess they don't want to have to bother hunters to come out on separate days and do one round at a time. One benefit of there being two rounds is that if you miss a friend or loved one's hunter round, perhaps from falling asleep watching other hunters go, they are likely about to go in the ring again in a round or two.

Hunters are also subjected to a number of other occasionally arcane elements of competition. One of the more defensible quirks is the handy round, which is a modified over fences course that tests, you guessed it, the hunter's handiness. What does it mean to be handy? We can rule out the definition "skillful with the hands" because horses don't have hands, last I checked.[15] Handiness refers more to "easily

---

[15] A centaur would almost certainly win every handy round and probably would be owned by Dr. Betsee Parker.

maneuvered" or how well the horse obeys the rider. Handy courses feature elements such as a jump that you trot over as well as approaches to jumps with tight turns or on an angle.. Sometimes it is a separately scored round, but in Hunter Derbies, the top competitors go on to a jump-off-like handy round which adds the two scores together to determine the winner. More importance is placed on the cumulative placements across all the classes in a division during a show weekend, where the top finishers are named champion (1st) and reserve champion (2nd). With these distinctions come cool tri-color ribbons: blue, red and yellow for champion and red, white and yellow for reserve champion.[16] They are also awarded in the jumper divisions but are somewhat less important.

The second element of hunter competition is the under saddle. This is when all of the class's competitors ride in a circle around the outside of the ring without going over jumps, like the world's least intimidating and most expensive biker gang. During the under saddle, judges tell riders, through the announcer, to go at a certain pace that changes throughout and score the round based on how well the horse moves across the ground. The equitation discipline has a similar element referred to as the flat class, where the judges focus more on the rider's ability to follow instructions. Because of all the people involved, the under saddle can become something of a traffic jam. You can get cut off by other riders, and some ambitious ones will also try to

---

[16] Seeing a picture of a rider on social media with a champion ribbon is much more of a sign that they're a baller than a blue 1st place ribbon. There are some low-level jumper classes that give everyone a blue ribbon just for going clear. Getting a champion ribbon at WEF is nearly impossible and means you are undoubtedly skilled and likely extremely wealthy.

maximize their time in front of the judge by lingering at that side then going back around the rest of the ring as quickly as possible. It can be simultaneously cutthroat and extremely boring. At the end, all the participants line up together with their backs facing the judges so they can read their numbers. They then announce the finishers, starting at the top. As riders are announced, they exit the ring, so if you place last you're left all alone in the ring waiting for them to call your name. This is the horse show world equivalent of being picked last in gym class.

Not to be outdone in ridiculous award presentation, the winners of the regular over fences classes are sometimes announced by a jog. In a jog, the rider must demonstrate to the judge that their horse is serviceably sound after jumping by leading it past them on foot with the horse trotting. The jog is done without the saddle and the rider does not have to be the one jogging with the horse. Only the top finishers are asked to jog. The jumper division only has a jog at the start of the show week for horses competing in FEI-rated classes. It is rare that a horse is not deemed sound by the jog, but it can be an amusing exercise. There is a bit of absurdity in having to actually jog while leading your horse to coax it to trot past the judges, and that you actually have to run for your ribbons. Some of the more entertaining moments I have had watching hunters are jogs where some horses have difficulty following their leaders and some leaders have difficulty following their horses. The most nonsensical part is that riders must jog their horses for both classes if they were top finishers in both. If you have demonstrated that your horse is sound to the judges, what is going to change in the two minutes between when they give out ribbons for the first class and the second? But, as you know, that's the way they've always done it.

In addition to a jog, some hunter divisions, especially those at the pony level, have a conformation class as well. A conformation class is similar to an animal breed show—the riders take their horses out into the ring in a line without a saddle and a judge walks by and examines each horse before scoring them on their appearance. More entertainment can be had here when riders, especially little girls, have difficulty presenting or getting their pony's attention when the judge comes by. The jog and the conformation greatly reinforce the idea of hunters as a beauty pageant, though they do add some little amounts of drama for people like me that have no idea what's going on.

As you are beginning to understand from the multitude of different elements of hunter competition, neophytes to the sport have very little hope when it comes to assessing how a hunter round is going or finished. Unless, of course, the horse stopped at a jump or knocked it over. The judges are looking for very small things like the horse's form over jumps, where it takes off and lands and on what foot it does so. There is no live scoring system, and many times after the round the score is not even announced, so you have no way to know how well the rider did unless you have a detailed understanding of the hunter minutiae. Even then, your assessment of the round may not match the judge's. This leads to many opportunities where, as previously mentioned, unknowledgeable loved ones congratulate riders on terrible rounds. Here are the biggest things to remember if you have no idea what is going on but are watching hunters because someone you know is competing in them:

- Listen for scores. If you are lucky, they will announce a score on a 100-point scale after a round. Anything above 75 is decent. Anything below 60 is not.
- Know your rider's show number. They usually wear it on their back on a big license plate-like card. Most competitions will only announce the show number when announcing the final placement, so if you don't know it, you will be late in realizing they have called out your rider.
- Figure out when the last jumps are for each round, so you know when to clap after each one. This can be done by watching riders go beforehand and seeing when they finish. Warning: the last jump will change in the second round, so be sure you know the last jump for both. If this is too difficult, just start clapping when a trainer claps or allow for a delay to be sure they are done. Bonus points if you develop your own distinctive cheer/whistle/clap.
- If no score is announced and you have no idea how they did, refrain from congratulating them. Follow the lead of the trainer or someone who actually knows how they performed.
- Don't fall asleep or die of boredom. Seek shade and stay hydrated.

A brief closing note on hunter competition: it is almost nonexistent outside of the US. The horses that compete in it are mostly European breeds, and fox hunting originated in Europe. But, for some reason, the hunter show jumping discipline that descended from it has only taken off in the states. Fox hunting in the US is still very much alive today, as I visited a few of its enclaves that hold hunter/jumper shows and experienced it firsthand. I have no answer for why the hunter discipline didn't catch on in Europe—all I can imagine is that they are as irritated as I am about having to do a second jog. As a result of it being only a national sport, the professional hunter scene is very small with very few large prize money events each year compared to the jumper ring, with very little crossover between the two disciplines at the highest level. There is no real hierarchy for rankings or skill among professional hunter riders other than accumulated prize money, which can be inflated greatly by the number of horses used and events entered. Compared to the jumper discipline, there are far fewer junior riders that aspire to be professional hunter riders. The vast majority are amateur or junior riders that do it because of tradition or because they like the horses and the style of competition (I would imagine). Somehow, almost three thousand words later, I cannot sufficiently explain the existence of the hunter discipline. It's just the way it's always been done.

CHAPTER FOUR

Equitation
Eternal Glory and Training Bills

There is no scene that epitomizes the idiosyncrasies of the A-circuit hunter/jumper scene more than equitation, or at its highest levels, "Big Eq." But before I wax poetic about my uninformed opinions on the discipline, here's some background. Equitation is the discipline where winners are determined by a subjective judging of the rider's form going around the course.[17] While there are equitation classes in which adults compete, the notable ones are reserved only for juniors. Unlike in the jumper and hunter disciplines where classes are divided by jump height or other factors, most equitation classes are only differentiated by their name and minute competition differences. The entry level equitation classes start at the 3' height, but most are around 3'6". There are four main equitation classes: Maclay, Medal, USEF Talent Search and WIHS. Maclay and Medal are referred to as such,

---

[17] The word equitation, or "eq" for short, can also refer to the rider's form and is frequently a subject of commentary on social media, e.g., "her eq is on point" or "my eq is trash."

while USEF Talent Search is either referred to as USET or Talent Search. I referred to WIHS, short for Washington International Horse Show (where the finals are held) as it sounds phonetically—like a person with an extreme lisp saying "wish," before being told that most people refer to it as The Washington. It took me quite a bit of time to wrap my head around these arbitrarily named and separated classes that ostensibly measure the same thing at the same level of difficulty. It would be like if there were a 1.20m junior jumping competition named Youth Jumpers and an identical competition with slightly different jump-off rules named Low Junior Jumpers and everyone competed in both. These classes are separated because they all correspond to a year-end equitation finals event. Each class at an individual show serves as a sort of qualifying round for the finals event that takes place at a specific location in the fall during a stretch of shows called indoors. Each equitation class has its own history and slight differences.

MACLAY

The Maclay is the oldest equitation class. It began in 1933 and is held annually at the National Horse Show. In its heyday, the show was a big shindig held at Madison Square Garden but has more recently been relegated to the rodeo-like Alltech Arena at the Kentucky Horse Park, taking place every year in the last weekend of October. It's sponsored by ASCPA, because founder Alfred Maclay, was a board member of that organization. The finals course features a huge, scary jump that spells out the letters ASPCA with gigantic As on both sides forming the standards. Because of its age, the Maclay is the most prestigious class—almost any rider would pick this equitation final as the most desirable to win. In Maclay qualifying classes, all riders participate in one round, then the top riders, usually 12 in a big class like at WEF, are called back for a flat class together before a winner is determined. At Maclay Finals, riders go around a course, then the top 30 or so are called back for a second day where they will compete in a flat class, then be narrowed down again for a second jumping class. After this, they will sometimes be narrowed down to a very small group of 2-4 where the judges will have them do something crazy like switch horses and complete a course. The courses can be either jumper courses or hunter courses.

MEDAL

The US Hunt Seat Medal Final, or the Medal, is the second oldest equitation class, established in 1937 by the then governing body of horse shows, which apparently saw all the attention the Maclay was getting and decided they needed to get in on the action. The official history is something about separating the Hunt Seat, Saddle Seat and Stock Seat competitors, but I don't fully comprehend that, so I'm going with my first reason. Medal Finals is held at the Pennsylvania National Horse Show in Harrisburg, PA, around the second week of October, and is probably the main reason why most of the competitors are at that show. The Medal is sponsored by Pessoa, a saddle company, and it is very similar to, if not slightly less prestigious than, the Maclay. They have the same jump height, can be held in a hunter or jumper ring, and both start with M and have ambitious-sounding names. The main difference between Medal and Maclay is the final deciding round. Instead of Maclay's flat class, the Medal's final round consists of a test in which riders are given a series of instructions about gait and jumps that they must perform around the course, then immediately execute them without consulting a trainer, or sometimes even watching their competitors. The test is one of the most compelling elements of equitation competition, especially for spectators, and probably a much better judge of the factors behind equitation scoring than a flat class. I make sure to encourage all equitation riders to talk to their horses about getting Medal tested.

USEF TALENT SEARCH

The most peculiar sounding is the USEF Talent Search, or just USET for short, an equitation final sanctioned by the governing body of US equestrian, USEF.[18] I always expect to see grizzled scouts in windbreakers in the stands at any Talent Search class because of its name. It is actually very different than the other three classes. First, it is only held on a jumper course, and the jump heights go up to 3'9" instead of the 3'6" maximum of all the other classes. Recently, they also added a mandatory water jump on the course, requiring a horse that can handle the tricky obstacle. It is also open to all riders 21 and under, not just junior riders. Strangely, even professionals meeting the age requirement can compete in it. USEF Talent Search is also unique in that it holds two different finals around the first week in October, an East final currently held in Gladstone, NJ and a West final currently held in San Juan Capistrano, CA, so there are two winners crowned each year. This is a bit misleading, as the East Final is considered the

---

[18] USEF strangely changed its name to "US Equestrian" as this was about to be printed, so I'm going to keep calling it that since it's still called USEF Talent Search right now. Thanks Murray.

more competitive final, because its talent pool is much larger. Making it even more difficult, the finals have three different phases: jumping, flat and gymnastics. It's sponsored by Platinum Performance, a supplement or something. Platinum Performance/USEF Show Jumping Talent Search doesn't exactly roll off the tongue like Pessoa Medal does. We are getting dangerously close to the show title complexity of the Sprint/Nextel Winston NASCAR Cup events with the Equitation sponsorships. The USET started it around 1965 as a way to encourage juniors who had already qualified for Medal and Maclay early in the year to continue doing equitation until finals. It is slightly less prestigious than Medal and Maclay because it is newer and different and is diminished somewhat by the geographical champion divide. Despite this, it is arguably the most difficult to win and the case could be made that its winners have a higher chance of professional success.

WIHS

The Washington International Horse Show Equitation Final is held at its namesake show, which takes place around the last week of October at the Verizon Center in Washington, D.C. The Washington, as it is called, is probably the least prestigious of the big four, being relatively new. Its main difference is that competition is in two phases at all qualifying shows and at the finals: a hunter phase and a jumper phase over their respective courses. It also has a very difficult qualifying requirement for the finals, with only 40 riders competing at the finals compared to the over 100 at the Medal and Maclay. Where the Maclay sometimes has riders switch horses in the finals, the Washington always does this in an event called a work-off. While the Washington isn't Medal or Maclay, they have shoehorned themselves into the Grand Slam of Equitation Finals in an impressive way, making sure that their show name is at every other big A-Circuit show with equitation classes.

So now that you know about the big four equitation finals, what's the point? What makes equitation so unique is that it has the most prestigious culminating championship for a junior rider. In the jumper division for juniors, there is the North American Junior and Young Riders championship, where a win is a nice resume addition but nothing that a top rider would feel is mandatory to attend. If you were talented enough, you would just start riding against professionals as a junior. The hunter division has junior hunter finals and Pony Finals, but are more fragmented by horse type. Equitation fills the void that these other disciplines have by giving riders a very clear and worthy goal to attempt with their riding. For some, just qualifying and riding in the championship events is enough, while others want their name etched in immortality as a winner of the event. And riders can only win each of the equitation finals once—after that you aren't allowed to compete in them. Because of this, there are no two-time winners of any single event, just winners of multiple equitation finals. A handful of riders have won three of them, but only one, Brianne Goutal in 2004 and 2005, has won all four.

What does winning an equitation championship get you besides a sense of accomplishment unmatched by any other you can attain as a junior? There is no prize money awarded in most equitation events and it is extremely costly, so monetary rewards are out. The show jumping governing body would probably answer this question by citing how a strong junior equitation program develops future champions in the sport by instilling a competitive environment where riders are encouraged to learn and perfect proper form and riding style. I remain a skeptic of this, as while being a formidable equitation rider will help you be a better rider in the professional jumper ring, it won't win you any Grand Prix events alone.[19] A comparative example would be if all major youth basketball tournaments were scored based not on baskets, but on the number of perfect passes and shot form throughout the game. Then, at 18, all the tournaments started playing the usual game of basketball supposedly using the techniques they honed in the youth leagues and rarely, if ever, played the old way ever again. The only logical arena for this sort of transition would be football, where they could somehow slowly introduce the contact as the players are older to avoid head injuries, but I think Texas would finally secede from the union if this transpired.

To me, the two main answers to "what's the point?" are—because it feels important and to a much lesser degree, to get into college. If you join a sport and someone in it says "my dream is to win Maclay finals" then you naturally assume that's something you should also do. A long time ago, someone decided these equitation finals were important, and over time that prestige has only increased in the absence of something else as revered in another discipline for juniors. For most this seems to be the motivating factor. For a smaller group, equitation performance serves as the main factor for being evaluated for a scholarship by one of the few schools

---

[19] In Europe there is no equitation at the junior level, and they seem to have no trouble producing fundamentally sound professional riders.

that has an NCAA equestrian program. This is because the competition at the college level is also in the equitation discipline. Never mind that most riders' parents will spend much more money on their child's equitation careers than the value of these partial scholarships to mostly large state schools, as you will learn later in the college equestrian chapter.

Because of its heightened level of importance, the equitation scene likely has the most distinctive culture on the A-circuit. More money and energy are thrown into it than imaginable, and for a good reason: it's subjective. Human judges determine the winners. As a result, the competition becomes unavoidably political. The hunter discipline has this same problem, but for the most part the stakes are much lower. In equitation, the judges cannot willfully ignore things like the reputation of the rider, their horse, or especially their trainer as they go around the ring. They are supposed to remain neutral and judge as if they have no previous knowledge of who they are seeing, but this is very difficult to do when you see the face or hear the cheer of Big Name Trainer X at the in-gate after their star client's round on the horse that won an equitation finals event last year. You could make the case that in the jumper division, the rider and horse are equally the most important keys to success; being a skilled rider and having a talented and capable horse are both required to reach the highest levels of competition. In the hunter division, the horse's ability can overshadow the rider's skill to a degree, as scoring is based on the performance of the horse. In equitation, I believe the trainer is at least as important as the rider or the horse. You would expect the rider to be the main focus because the judging is supposed to be based solely on their performance. But the trainer is the one who coaches the rider on how to do what the judges want, puts them on a horse that is going to give them the best chance of success and puts their name, face and reputation behind that rider for the judges. The reason I believe this is found in the results: since 2003 all the winners of Maclay and Medal Finals have come only from four different training barns: Beacon Hill (run by Stacia and formerly Frank Madden), Heritage (run by Andre Dignelli), North Run (run by Missy Clark and John Brennan) and Don Stewart's barn. Since they have all been active over the last 25 or so years, they have trained over 80% of the winners of these events, including 50 of the 52 winners in the past 13 years. At least in the modern era, it has proven almost impossible to win an equitation final without one of these Big Name Trainers, or "BNTs" in your corner, as illustrated by the chart on the next page.

	Maclay	Medal	USET East	WIHS
2016	DS	BH	BH	DS
2015	NR	DS	HE	HE
2014	HE	DS	HE	NR
2013	HE	HE	NR	BH
2012	HE	DS	HE	BH
2011	DS	HE	HE	QH/BH
2010	NR	NR		HE
2009	NR	BH	HE	HE
2008	BH	NR	BH	
2007	NR	NR	BH	BH
2006	HE	HE	NR	NR
2005	BH	BH	NR	NR
2004	QH	QH	BH	BH
2003		DS	NR	HE
2002	DS	NR	NR	
2001	NR		QH	
2000		NR	NR	
1999	NR	NR	QH	HE
1998	NR	HE		NR
1997	QH/BH	NR	HE	
1996	NR	QH	QH	

HE = Heritage
BH = Beacon Hill
NR = North Run
DS = Don Stewart
QH = Quiet Hill

I stop short of using this as definitive evidence that the system favors only riders who pay to be at a top barn and have the best chance to win a subjective competition. There are a number of factors behind why the results have played out the way they have. First, they could be because these trainers are simply very good at what they do. They know what it takes to win and they are able to guide a steady stream of new talent to victory over the course of time. A second factor is that in at least a few cases, some of these barns will swoop in and start training promising riders shortly before the finals, usually at a discount, so if they win they have the prestige attached to their barns. This is not to say that their training presence doesn't affect the rider's chances of winning. However, were the results different and not so overwhelmingly favoring these trainers as a necessity to victory, then I would be less inclined to believe it wasn't a large factor. The majority of the participants in these events, with the exception of USET East Finals and WIHS Finals, are not from these top barns. The 2015 USET East Finals, which lists the trainer along with all the participants, had 37 of its 61 competitors from the top four barns. However, the top 4 barns were the only ones represented in the top 18 placings. At bigger events, like Maclay and Medal finals with up to 130 participants, the top four barns make up a much smaller proportion of the overall competitor pool but still train a majority of the finalists. In the 2015 Maclay, of the 30 invited back to the second day, 19 were from the top barns, as well as 7 of the top 10 finishers. The 2015 Medal had 9 of the top 10 represented by the top 4 barns, as well. So, not only are the winners from these top barns, but a disproportionate number of the finalists are as well.

The other factor involved in this is that training at these dominating barns is not cheap. Board alone costs upwards of $3,500 a month, and that does not include what will be an extremely expensive lease for (likely) multiple equitation horses as well as show costs. Unless you somehow get very lucky and have a show barn attach itself to you at a small price as you are on the way up, seriously competing for an equitation final will be costly. This is my main problem with equitation finals and the discipline in general. If it is billed as the ultimate goal and training for young and up and coming equestrians, why is success in it so predicated by money and whom you train with? It could be an opportunity for the sport to mitigate the relationship wealth has with success in a certain area, but instead it goes down the other path. Many riders enter equitation because they want to use their riding ability to earn a college scholarship. Most are quickly faced with the fact that they have no chance of competing against riders with significantly more money or resources.

I did not attend any equitation finals and my only experience watching the discipline was in the smaller qualifying classes. I had slightly more of an idea of what was going on than a hunter round, but still was fairly clueless as to how a round was going until the judge mercifully announced the score. Despite this, even at these smaller events there was a palpable sense of competitive intensity. All of these top barns compete against each other at WEF and a few other shows before purposefully splitting up in the summer. Seeing them all go against each other was very exciting during my travels. However, it lost its luster for me when I realized how much money went into it and how little chance there was of someone without the top training succeeding at what is regarded as the most important prize for young riders. Equitation ends up unfortunately epitomizing the outsider's perspective on horse showing: that it is the exclusive and political sport of the wealthy.

CHAPTER FIVE

Professionals
How People Actually Do This for a Living

There are two worlds on the A-circuit, the junior/amateur one and the professional one. The larger groups of riders are under 18 (juniors) or riders who do not attempt to make a living riding (amateurs), either because they have another job and do it for fun or they have the resources and the time. Once you declare as a professional, you are allowed to be sponsored and make money from the sport via training or other methods. There are two distinct levels at which professionals compete. The higher level sees them traveling to only the biggest shows around the world, with the Americans going to a few more shows in North America that cross over with the lower level professionals competing only in the states. The closest sport I can compare the higher level professional show jumping scene to is tennis. It is mostly individual, personality driven and spread around a number of different nations with competitions internationally. Here is a primer on the distinctive elements of professional show jumping that are found in very few other sports.

MAKING MONEY

The basic distinction between a professional and an amateur is their ability to profit on the sport. They can earn prize money, with purses stretching into the hundreds of thousands (which amateurs can also earn). However, for all but maybe three of the top American riders, the prize money they win will not offset their expenses. In some cases, the prize money will be split between riders and owners of the horse. There are sponsorships for riders, but these ordinarily offset the costs associated with their products. There are no lifetime Nike deals like LeBron's. Most of the money made as a professional show jumper is through two avenues: training and buying and selling horses. Professionals charge fees for lessons, for boarding at their barns and for instruction during shows. Most of the money made in the sport comes from the expenses paid by the majority of juniors, amateurs and even other professionals who are sinking money into it. Some professionals are like juniors and amateurs: they have no need to make money off the sport because they are independently wealthy. Despite the lure of prize money for amateur and junior classes, for most riders there is no feasible way to fully offset their considerable expenses riding under those classifications. I will go in to the gory details of costs in a later chapter.

TRAINING

A good portion of professional riders are also trainers to junior, amateur or even other professional riders. This involves giving them regular lessons that prepare them for showing, then handling showing day duties such as walking the course with the rider, setting jumps in the schooling ring, and giving counsel after a round. For the riders, a trainer is likely the most important relationship they will have in the sport. The trainer helps you decide what kind of horse to ride, what classes to show in, what tack to use and basically every major detail related to your riding. Riders can have a wide range of emotions toward their trainers. Some regard them as a necessary evil and are nonchalant about their interactions with them. Others are star-struck despite interacting with them regularly. My girlfriend personally spends far more time crafting text messages to her trainer than she does to me. Trainers can also be notoriously difficult to communicate with and not technologically literate, leading to text exchanges like this:

Rider: Should I get to the barn tomorrow at 7:30 or 9?
Trainer: Yes correct

On the other side, trainers often find themselves providing much more than just equine training to their clients. They can become a sort of therapist, dealing with all of their riders' issues and quirks on a daily basis. I personally appreciate trainers that do this, as it leaves less of these duties for horse show boyfriends to assume.

SUCCESS

With any sport, the key to evaluating and enjoying it as a spectator is determining its unique measurements and requirements for success. In football, you need to win the

Super Bowl, and to do that you need (among other things) to have the best team comprised of players who are the best at passing, running and defending. We place inordinate emphasis on a year-end tournament of the best teams or players, and in order to be the best you have to possess certain physical and mental talents. Individual sports, like tennis or golf, are not defined or measured by an annual championship. They have four major yearly events determining the best of the sport. Show jumping is very different. Only in junior equitation in the US is there a similar system to tennis and golf, with four major finals events that are more heavily weighted. At the professional level, there is no widely accepted measure of success. The Grand Prix events sanctioned by the world governing body of equestrian, the FEI, are designated by stars from 2 to 5, with a 5* being the hardest event with the most prize money. But there is a very different level of prestige attached to each event, affected by where events take place, based on their histories and competition. None are far and away more important than the others so as to be labeled major yearly events. There are really only three events that are viewed as more important than the rest, and two only happen once every four years: The Olympics and World Equestrian Games. The other, the World Cup final, takes place yearly. These events are competed in and scored differently than the normal FEI Grand Prix competition throughout the year, so in some cases a different type of horse is more suitable for one than the other. I will go into more detail about these in the next section, but the fact that there is so much variability in the results and that these events are so infrequent may not make them reliable indicators of success. One of the top show jumpers in the sport could very easily have not won or placed at any of these top three events.[20] There are ranking systems in place for FEI events and USEF events (the governing body of US Equestrian), and are weighted towards riders that are able to compete more frequently or win at less competitive events. These events are seen less as referendums on the top talent but as general measures of rider competence. The only consistent measure seems to be the number of wins or top placings at large Grand Prix or Nations Cup events over a period of time.

The requirements for success at the highest level of the sport are equally subjective, because of all of the variables of the horses ridden. Your success as a rider is inalterably tied to the horses you ride, making it far less of a meritocracy than other sports. In very few, if any other sports, does having access to better equipment determine your success. While you have to have some natural ability to make it to the highest level of competition, you can be the most talented rider in the world but not have the horses that allow you to compete at the highest level. This requirement introduces several necessary elements to success: money, personal relationships and reputation. The money part is simple. If you can afford the best horses and the best training, you are limited only by your own ability and to a small extent, luck. As I will discuss in the Big Names section, almost all of the up-and-coming professional American riders are wealthy, making it easier for them to reach that level at a younger age. For those that do not have infinite capital at their disposal, reputation and

---

[20] Only one rider has managed to win all three in a career (Rodrigo Pessoa), and only because the rider who finished ahead of him at the Olympics was disqualified months later after his horse tested positive for a banned substance.

relationships outside of the ring become just as important as ability in the ring. This is because you are largely dependent on other people to own and finance your horses. This can be in the form of clients, who are junior or amateur riders that, as a stipulation of training with you, provide you with a Grand Prix level horse to ride. Other riders use horses owned by absentee owners who do not ride but want to participate in the sport. While winning in the ring can help these things happen, forging relationships at horse shows is a key element, as the more connections you have the more likely you are to find a match with a wealthy client or owner wanting to support your career. In some ways, this can be a frustrating element of a sport that validates its outside perception as a sport for the wealthy. It is nearly impossible to succeed at the highest levels without money from the rider or wealthy backers. Even at the junior or amateur level, having money gives you a great advantage over the competition and can compensate for average rider ability. To me it seems odd that being able to talk about yourself and your skill can be just as important as being able to judge distances in the ring when it comes to success, but it's a far cry from the hunter and dressage world where reputation can literally affect your score in competition.

CHAMPIONSHIPS

There are three events that stand out as jumping career landmarks above the others, in order of importance: The Olympics, the World Equestrian Games, and the World Cup Final. The Olympics are what you think they are, the summer games held every four years with the jumping, eventing and dressage disciplines. This is the only time most people in the US are aware people do something with horses other than race them. They mostly take this time to make fun of dressage and talk about how equestrian events shouldn't be in the Olympics.[21] The World Equestrian Games were started in 1990 and are held every four years halfway between the Olympics (sort of like soccer's World Cup). They include eight equestrian disciplines including the Olympic three and other crazy ones like driving, reining, endurance and vaulting. The World Cup Final is held annually in April and was started in 1978. It includes only dressage and show jumping, which are frequently held at different locations.

Equestrian events have been part of the Olympics since 1900, and its early history is fairly amusing. In 1900, there were all sorts of random disciplines like vaulting, mail-coach driving and long jump. In 1904 when the Olympics moved to the US, equestrian events were mysteriously dropped.[22] Luckily, and I couldn't make this up if I tried, equestrian events returned to the Olympics thanks to Count Clarence von Rosen, Master of the Horse to the King of Sweden and a member of the International Olympic Committee. So he is who we have to thank for show jumping at the Olympics today, and maybe for the sport's international popularity. Not going to lie, I would take Count Clarence von Rosen over Walter Camp or James Naismith any day. They didn't get their stuff together in time for the 1908 Olympics, so equestrian events were held again at the 1912 Olympics and persisted

---

[21] I'm an NBA fan and I would say it belongs more than basketball. The competition is way more exciting than watching the US dominate Angola.

[22] I say mysteriously because some basic googling yielded no answers as to why. The horsey-est president ever, Teddy Roosevelt, was in office, so you'd think he might have championed the sport.

until the present-day. Until 1952, only "commissioned officers and gentlemen" were permitted to compete in the equestrian events at the Olympics.[23] This restriction had the added effect of the 1932 and 1936 individual gold medal winners dying some 10 years later at Iwo Jima and the Eastern front in the Soviet Union respectively. I wouldn't be opposed to this restriction today if only to see McLain and Kent in Special Forces fatigues.

The World Equestrian Games, or WEG, are relatively new and the result of a consolidation of the championships of several different equestrian disciplines. It is a sort of equestrian Olympics, occurring every four years with a rotating host city and put on by the governing equestrian sport body, the International Federation for Equestrian sports, or FEI. It contains most of the disciplines recognized by the FEI in addition to the three recognized in the Olympics. Since its start in 1990, it has been held in various locations in Europe except in 2010, when it was held in Lexington, Kentucky. The WEG show jumping competition doesn't have the prestige of the Olympics but is still a very big deal to win because it is only held once every four years and attracts all the best competitors.

The World Cup Final is the annual championship sanctioned by FEI. It is the only event of the three where riders qualify based on FEI events throughout the year.[24] At WEG and the Olympics, nations qualify based on their zones and then the chef d'equipe, or captain of the nations' teams, picks the riders, usually based on evaluation at certain

---

[23] I have no idea what qualified one as a gentleman, but if anyone finds out please let me know so I can aspire to be one.

Olympic-like competitions. The World Cup Final also only has an individual component, where the other two events have both a team and individual competition. It has been held mostly in Europe or the United States since its inception in 1979. In recent years it has most frequently been held in Las Vegas when it comes to the US.

The Olympics and WEG operate under a different type of scoring than most Grand Prix events, with an individual championship and a team championship. The team championship scoring is often referred to as Nations Cup scoring because it is also used at Nations Cup events, where teams from different countries compete at smaller competitions throughout the year. The main factor in this scoring are penalties or faults accrued from knocking a rail down or exceeding the time allowed around the course. Winners are determined by whoever accumulates the fewest faults. In the event of a tie a jump-off is held where speed is a factor. I will discuss more of my opinions about this format and my first experience with it in the chapter on the Young Riders' championship.

GENDER & RELATIONSHIPS

The equestrian sport is one of the few where men and women compete against one another. Most people will tell you that one gender does not have any sort of advantage over the other. Women completely outnumber men by a wide margin at the non-professional levels. As I write this, 45 of the top 50 riders in the US Under 25 rankings are female, and in the US Children's Jumper rankings, all of the top 50 riders are female. However, in the current US professional rankings, only 30 of the 50 are female. The hunter side is similar, with 32 of the top 50 professional money winners of the last 10 years being female despite there being virtually no male riders in the top placings in junior hunter finals classes. I have no definitive answers to explain this, but what I have gathered is that in the US as a junior, it is considered much more of sport for females, and the collegiate teams are exclusively female. The males who do compete as juniors seem to have a much higher likelihood of becoming professionals than do females, perhaps because they may be more determined competitors in a primarily female sport.

The disparity changes drastically outside of the US: in the world rankings, only 10 of the current top 50 are female. At the junior levels internationally, male and female participation is almost equal. The US is probably the most female-centric equestrian nation, frequently competing with all-female Nations Cup teams professionally and sending what is likely the only all-female Olympic team to Sydney in 2000. Internationally, even in areas outside of Europe, it is much more of a recognized sport among the general public, with Grand Prix events frequently on television. Probably as a result of this awareness, it is more comparable to a sport like baseball in the United States, with males being encouraged to do it at a young age and more frequently doing it professionally as a means of making a living.

Romantic relationships between participants in the sport are exceedingly common, likely because of the co-existence of male and female athletes in competition, the grueling schedule and the all-encompassing lifestyle. In other sports, like tennis, you hear of the occasional Agassi/Graf union, but it seems like the majority of people competing in A-circuit show jumping have a partner in it as well. There can be many different dynamics at work: both can be professional riders with separate or joint businesses; one can be professional and one amateur; or, one can be a rider and one can be a trainer or involved in some other way. It is not unheard of for trainers to date or end up marrying a riding client, sometimes even while said trainer is already married. The excessive closeness of the sport continues to its progeny. Large numbers of junior or young professional riders have parents that are or were involved in the sport. A few others get involved either because they are wealthy or because they love horses, but the vast majority share a last name with a well-known professional or amateur rider. This leads me to think of juniors in Harry Potter wizarding terms—are you a pure-blood (both of your parents into show jumping), half-blood (one of them), or muggle-born (neither of them). Muggle-borns are as rare at Hogwarts as they are at WEF.

The unequal gender participation causes males in the sport to be in very high demand, further exacerbated by the disproportionately higher number of gay male riders in the sport. Being a straight male rider must feel a little like being on The Bachelor—there are no roses but the 1:30 gender ratio is about right. There is a steady stream of international male riders to woo (namely the Irish and South American ones), but they do not make a dent in the imbalance. Nowhere is it more prevalent than at the junior level. I fear American junior male riders (all 10 or so of them) might develop some sort of personality disorder being so overwhelmed by romantic interests on a regular basis. I know that if I have a son and he is having trouble with the ladies as a teenager, he's getting riding lessons for his birthday.

INTERNATIONAL REPRESENTATION

There is no single dominating nation in show jumping today. Historically, Germany probably has produced the most winners, but there is parity among nations today. Currently 17 different nations are in the top 50 rankings and 28 in the top 100. The US and Germany have the most in the top 50, with 6 each, followed by France and Belgium (5), Great Britain, Ireland and Switzerland (4) and the Netherlands (3). The six most recent winners of individual gold at the Olympics are from six different nations, and the six most recent team gold winners are from four different nations. The upper-tier of show jumping nations come from Western Europe, US, Canada and Brazil, with smaller notable participation from Argentina, Colombia, Venezuela, Saudi Arabia and Qatar. The history of show jumping is deeply rooted in Europe, with most of the show jumping horse breeds originating there.

While some countries' Olympic teams are very difficult to make because of the breadth and quality of competitors from each nation, the end results and world rankings are very diverse, largely because of the unpredictability of the sport. It is difficult to consistently win events because of the variability in performance from round to round. A horse and rider combination having the smallest of mistakes can cost them a win, and with a good portion of the competitors at any major event capable of winning, a better rider can frequently be beaten by a less accomplished or skilled one. This contrasts with subjective scoring events like dressage, where small mistakes can affect a judge's overall score but not completely derail a rider's chances of winning or put him or her in a position to lose to lesser competition. In a related story, Germany has won team gold at the Olympics in dressage 8 out of the last 9 times.

AGE

There is no particular peak age range in show jumping. Juniors can start competing in Grand Prix events at 13, in bigger events at around 17, and can turn professional at 18. Riders can continue competing into their 60s successfully. The winner of the 2016 Olympic Individual Gold, Nick Skelton, was 58 years old at the time and previously had a supposed career-ending neck injury and hip replacement. Generally, riders are in top form from their mid 30s to their mid 40s, since experience seems to play a much greater role than physical ability in success at the highest level. The physical attributes that allow one to ride don't seem to diminish greatly during this age period. They are far less important than the planning and knowledge involved from doing the sport at a professional level for a long period of time. While there have been a few moments of younger riders attaining spots on the national teams for the biggest events, very few of the top ranked riders are under 30.

HORSE PARTNERSHIPS

In thoroughbred racing, the horses are very much the central competitors with the riders being secondary players. Show jumping is much more focused on the rider and the rider/horse partnership—and riders are never, ever called jockeys. If you hear someone call a show jumping rider a jockey, they are either a total noob or such a rich owner that they forgot which kind of horse sport they were spending a lot of money on at the time. Only in the hunter ring is the focus slightly more horse-centric because the judging is based on their form. Winners are announced rider first, then horse second and the important rankings are by rider. Riders have multiple horses, many times competing against themselves in the same event. However, the top jumper horses are followed with the same interest as a top thoroughbred, just more as a partnership with their current rider. In the selection for team events like the Olympics or Nations Cup, consideration is given not just to the rider but to the ability of their eligible horses. You could be the best rider in the US, but if you didn't have an Olympic level horse to ride, you won't be going to the Olympics. It is rare that a horse will stay with one professional rider for the majority of its competitive lifespan. Frequently they will be sold to other professionals or amateurs, thus beginning a new partnership.

CHAPTER SIX

The Big Names
They All Sound Like They Jump Horses

The big names in American show jumping fall into two categories: people you have never heard of with amusingly unique names well-suited to show jumping; or, people with famous last names. Because it is a sport that requires a lot of money, you will see quite a few famous and wealthy families' progeny competing. If a last name sounds familiar, it usually is the daughter of that famous person: Bloomberg, Springsteen, Gates, Jobs.[25] An equal number of riders come from wealthy families who are unfamiliar to the general public: CEOs, founders of asset management companies, hedge funds, and the like. Part of the fun of being a horse show boyfriend is tracking down the money behind all the riders and then attempting, in vain, to figure out how to emulate their success. On the other side of the spectrum are the well-known professional riders. Despite being covered

---

[25] Some do sneak up on you: I had been watching a junior rider with the last name of Michaels for months before I made the connection that she was the daughter of Lorne Michaels, creator of Saturday Night Live.

with a helmet and watched from a distance, spectators learn about and develop feelings for the top professionals, based on their unique riding style and personality. Here is a brief overview of who you should know.

George Morris is arguably the most famous American in show jumping. The more I learn about him the more enigmatic and difficult it is to describe his status. He is generally recognized as one of the most reputable trainers in the sport. He is almost 80 years old and most recently served as the chef d'equipe for the US Olympic teams. As a rider at the age of 14, he was the youngest to win Maclay finals and he was one of the top American riders in the 1960s. He will likely be the first to admit that his riding accomplishments were at a time when it was easier to achieve them and are secondary to his training career. He has written a number of books on equitation and riding that are generally regarded as the best educational tools in the sport. He is always in demand for riding clinics and has trained numerous Olympians. His trademarks include his encyclopedic knowledge of the sport, his emphasis on the basics in training and his acerbic commentary. During my travels, Breyer introduced a George Morris action figure that spoke a number of his phrases, such as "you're very beautiful, I hope you have a brain" and "in horsemanship, there's a right and a wrong. Darlings, I have no time for wrong." I had the pleasure of meeting George at a friends' barn while he was giving them a lesson. Everyone present at the lesson was mostly terrified as he shouted barely discernible instructions from a megaphone. I did manage to win his approval by promptly picking out the ring and staying out of the way. He would later meet my girlfriend in the barn and was somewhat taken with her, offering the greeting of a kiss on the hand and then continuing up her arm. He then turned to me and asked, "How could a blind squirrel such as you find an acorn so beautiful as this?" Clearly, there is no denying his expertise both in and out of the ring. I do wonder to what degree he is more Simon Cowell: popular more because of his personality and reputation. You can't quantify his influence on his students' success, but his reputation is easily the most distinguished in the sport.[26]

McLain Ward might have the most amusingly suitable name for a show jumping professional. Now just over 40, he is probably the most successful American rider over the last decade, due to both his talent and opportunities. You would be hard pressed to find a rider who has been better positioned in the sport from a very early age, and someone who has worked harder to get to the top level. He won both USEF Talent Search and Medal Finals at the age of 14, became the youngest rider to win $1 million in prize money at 22, and has more recently competed for the US at the last four Olympics, winning team gold in 2004 and 2008. McLain's riding style is characterized by his meticulous preparation and perfectionist in-ring performance. You will very rarely see him with his hands, feet or position incorrect going around a course. McLain was probably the most dominant rider I saw in person during my first year watching show jumping. He defied the logical variance of show jumping by constantly winning big events more often than his peers. Every time he had a rail down it seemed stunning, even though it is a regular

---

[26] One of my other favorite things about George is that he frequently wears rust-colored breeches to the show, which my girlfriend says went out of style about when we were born. If I ever attempt to ride, I'm only doing it in rust-colored breeches.

occurrence for many riders. This is in part due to his skill, but also to his very high quality string of horses, many of which are owned by Hunter Harrison (CEO of Canadian Pacific Railway) and his aptly named Double H Farm. My most memorable McLain moment was after he won a 5-star event at WEF in 2016. He was posing with the winner of the media betting pool who picked him after the press conference and he jokingly said, "don't bet against me!" After watching him for a year, I wouldn't dare.

Much like McLain, the other big names of show jumping are often referred to by their first names in a "LeBron" way, but no one has the iconic first name like Beezie Madden. Beezie, short for Elizabeth, is in her early 50s and unquestionably the best and most popular female American rider. I learned early on that the throngs of girls that compete in show jumping as juniors regard Beezie as their riding idol above everyone else. Beezie was also part of the 2004 and 2008 US gold medal Olympic teams with McLain, and many of her big accomplishments were also firsts for a woman at the time—top 3 world ranking and the $1 million prize money mark. Beezie is coached by and runs a farm with her husband, John Madden. That's right—in the horse world, the John Madden people refer to is the trainer, not the football personality.[27] Beezie is best known in the ring for having ice water in her veins—she is always totally unfazed by the stakes of an event and is frequently in the anchor position for the US in team competition. Some also would say that Beezie is the most talented of the top American riders because of her

---

[27] It would be great to hear football John Madden commentate a Grand Prix. He would draw out the inside turn on a telestrator while saying "That horse hit the stride and BOOM! over the jump."

unique ability to ride the horse in a way that is best for them rather than conforming them to her style. Somehow during my year watching her, I managed to not see Beezie win one event in person. I can't say whether this was a down year overall for her and her horses, but I could certainly see why she has the profound admiration of other riders.

Beezie and McLain have been American fixtures in the sport for some time. Only recently have they been joined by a third powerhouse rider that would constitute something of an American Big 3: Kent Farrington. I know—another of-course-he-rides-horses name.[28] Despite his name, Kent did not come from show jumping progeny as most professionals do—he started out riding carriage horses outside Chicago. He quickly found his way to jumping and met the luminaries behind it like George Morris and Andre Dignelli. Now in his 30s, Kent won a number of Grand Prix events in the 2000s and has only recently vaulted into the Beezie/McLain superstar category, winning numerous events and placing 5th in the individual competition at the 2016 Olympics. Kent is like the Leonardo DiCaprio of the show jumping world to the masses of girls competing at the junior level—and he even looks a bit like him. To me, his defining characteristic in the ring is that he is a very exciting professional rider to watch in a jump off. If my life depended on picking one rider to get on a random horse and win a jump off, I would pick Kent. He is blazingly fast and sees and executes angles and turns few others are able to do on a regular basis. I watched Kent win again and again in my year on the A-circuit and I knew that any event he entered would be exciting.

---

[28] More examples: Todd Minikus, Hardin Towell, Adrienne Sternlicht, Hunt Tosh.

There are a number of other accomplished American riders that are not the up-and-coming professionals I will highlight later. One is worth mentioning because of her sheer uniqueness. Margie Goldstein-Engle is in her late 50s and is 5'1" tall. She rode for the US on the 2000 Olympic team and while she is in the twilight of her accomplished career, she remains both indestructible and gregarious. She has broken numerous bones and even hurt her foot so badly in 1991 that doctors told her she would likely not walk normally again. She was riding again in a week and was competing in ten weeks. She is still competing at a high level at an age when many of her contemporaries have retired. She was also named to the short list for the 2016 Olympic team. One of my favorite pictures during my travels was at New Albany with Margie walking to the ring with two other American riders who are both laughing at something she has said. I had the pleasure of talking to her after a Grand Prix win at Tryon, and I offhandedly mentioned that a few friends and I had done a betting pool on the event and one of them had correctly picked her, and she insisted on recording a funny video message thanking him for picking her and propelling her to victory. Most notably, while growing up, my girlfriend (also vertically challenged) had a poster of Margie on her wall and has always been a fan.

There are quite a few up-and-coming professional American riders between 18 and their early 30s. Most of them have two things in common: they are female and very wealthy. This list starts with the rider always referenced in any outside world story on show jumping: Georgina Bloomberg. Georgina is on the older end of the group and is probably the most familiar equestrian professional due to her father, Mike Bloomberg, founder of Bloomberg News and the former mayor of New York City. She has had a good amount of success in the ring, winning a number of bigger Grand Prix events and competing for the US in Nations Cup competition and at the Pan-Am Games in 2015. I talk more about meeting Georgina in person in the Central Park chapter, but it is worth mentioning that she has used her fame and status as a professional athlete admirably, starting a philanthropic organization dedicated to pet adoption and another that aims to make riding apparel more accessible to those in need. With her small, adorable toddler, philanthropic efforts and riding skill, Georgina is something of a Disney equestrian princess to the masses of junior riders to emulate.

The other up-and-coming riders, outside of Jessica Springsteen, do not have as familiar names but all come from wealthy families. Two bigger names are Reed Kessler and Lucy Davis, who competed in the 2012 and 2016 Olympics, respectively, on the US team. Reed did so at the age of 18 and Lucy at the age of 23. Both were much younger than their teammates, but accelerated their development with the help of fantastic horses and training. It seems they are indicative of a new era in show jumping where all 20-something professional riders must have unlimited financial capital to achieve meaningful success.[29] A part of me wonders if the financial homogeneity of the next generation of American show jumping stars is the best outcome for the sport. The

---

[29] In keeping with my interest in researching the financial backgrounds of wealthy riders, Lucy's father is the CEO of a large cap value fund, something I don't have nearly enough money to explain. Reed's father, Murray Kessler, recently became president of USEF and is probably most famous for smoking an e-cigarette on the floor of the NYSE during his time as CEO of Lorillard Tobacco.

current crop of top professionals seems to be much more diverse in economic and geographic background as well as personality.

One last 20-something rider worth mentioning is Brianne Goutal. She is 28, and like most other young professionals, has financial resources and hails from the northeast. Brianne had one of the most successful junior careers in show jumping. At the age of 16 in 2004, she won the WIHS and USET Talent Search East equitation finals, and then in 2005 she won both the Maclay and Medal finals, in addition to team and individual gold at the Young Riders championships. She is still the only rider to win all four equitation finals, and she did it with a year of junior eligibility left.[30] She also had great success in the hunter ring. In the ten years since, Brianne has won gold in Nations Cup events, won Grand Prix events, established a solid training business and qualified for World Cup Finals in 2008 and 2011. However, she has not made any of the US teams in the major competitions and has battled a few injuries during her time as a professional. In another sport this might resemble a junior phenom who has yet to make it big at the professional level, but this generalization does not apply to show jumping or Brianne in particular. Any of her contemporaries will tell you that she is a once-in-a-generation talent at show jumping. As someone new to the sport, it is difficult for me to grasp why she has not qualified for or had the success at big events that Reed and Lucy have. That she does not compete as much as them or have as strong a string of horses leads me to believe it is

---

[30] She even had a reality show on Animal Planet following her and her barn in the lead up to the final one for her to win, the 2005 Maclay, and she still won despite the pressure.

more her choice than her inability to do so. It may be that she can pick and choose what she wants to get out of the sport and might not feel the need to reach what some would consider the highest benchmarks of professional show jumping. It's not exactly Michael Jordan deciding to play baseball, but it does feel a little like I am missing out on watching a top rider perform at the highest level. I may be reading too much into Brianne's career, but as a new fan of the sport it does make me wonder how far her extraordinary talent would carry her. I also should mention Brianne is the only rider in this chapter that randomly struck up a conversation with me at a horse show. That counts for something since I was a random non-horseperson with a camera standing ringside and she's won all four eq finals.

Speaking of potential talent, perhaps the rider with the most intriguing and promising future is Victoria Colvin. During my year on the A-circuit, she was completing her final year of a successful junior career rivaling that of Brianne Goutal. Tori, as she is commonly known, stands out because she does not come from a very wealthy family. Her father is a farrier and her mother was a barn manager. What has made her junior career so exceptional is that she has dominated in all three disciplines of show jumping: jumpers, hunters, and equitation. Very rarely do juniors even compete in all three, let alone have success in them. She won the first Grand Prix she entered at 13 and frequently dominated the U25 and High junior classes at major shows in the jumper ring. She won basically every hunter accolade possible during her junior career including the biggest event at WEF—the Hunter Spectacular—three years in a row. Her equitation career was almost as impressive as Brianne's. She won three of the equitation finals, missing out only on Medal finals. By chance, Tori was at a majority of the shows I attended on my A-circuit odyssey, and it seemed like she won more often than she didn't, which is basically impossible in show jumping. She had girls coming to the shows just to see her ride in person. It felt like I was watching LeBron in his final year of high school. She was so dominant to the point that even when I had no idea what I was watching in the beginning, I knew that she was good. She cut corners in jump-offs like Kent and rode perfect handy hunter and equitation rounds over and over. Tori is now a professional and has won a few smaller Grand Prix events and is still competing and winning in the hunter ring (something other professionals also never do). Her talent and potential is endless, but nothing is guaranteed. In some ways, her future success will be a litmus test for if unlimited personal wealth is required to have top professional success in show jumping. She has attracted wealthy owners and backers with her talent, but it remains to be seen if this path that other professionals have taken will be successful in today's show jumping landscape. It seems that if Tori can't do it, no one can. I have no idea if she'll be the next Beezie or the first true top crossover professional hunter and jumper rider, but I can't wait to find out.

CHAPTER SEVEN

College Equestrian
Or How to Maybe Break Even Riding

I am going to diverge briefly to discuss a world I did not directly experience during my A-circuit travels but which loomed large in the future plans of riders I met along the way: riding for college teams. Like many other sports, riders often dream of continuing their competition in official collegiate sport. Most promising professional riders will forgo this and show around their college schedule (usually while attending an Ivy or Stanford). A few riders on collegiate teams will become professionals, but the vast majority are looking to continue riding while earning a portion of a scholarship. College equestrian is unique to the sport because of its team-first basis and even-handed competition.

Scholarship-based college equestrian started in 1996 when Fresno State was faced with a Title IX imbalance and needed to create an additional women's sports team. Most programs had added a women's crew team because of the relatively low cost and potential for attracting a high number of athletes, but Fresno State had no water source nearby. So, instead of building a lake, they started a varsity equestrian program and were met with a response that surpassed their expectations. That's right—the lack of a lake in arid central California is mostly to thank for the modern varsity college equestrian scene. Today, there are about 18 Division I teams in the NCEA, the governing body for NCAA college equestrian. There is also the IHSA, the governing body of the sport, at the club level which has over 360 colleges across the US and Canada that participate. A few random schools like Savannah College of Art and Design have an ISHA program that rivals an NCEA program.[31] However, there is usually a sizable gap between the two program levels. As with Fresno State, these NCEA teams count towards the Title IX laws requiring equal opportunities of male and female athletes at each school. By having women's equestrian, this allows them to balance out the much larger football programs. The 18-ish[32] NCEA teams are a melange of different schools: 4 from the SEC (Auburn, Georgia, South Carolina and Texas A&M),[33] 4 from the Big 12 (Kansas State, Oklahoma State, TCU and Baylor) and a few from the southwest and two Ivies. The competition has been dominated by the SEC schools—they have won every overall national championship since they started holding one in 2002. Most schools offer 15 scholarships for the riders which are split amongst all the non-walk-on riders. This means a rider could have up to 50% of a full scholarship, but it is usually closer to 25%. Not the payout a parent might be looking for

---

[31] SCAD also weirdly offers B.A.s in Equestrian Studies. I can't fathom paying $45k a year to learn course and barn design surrounded by artsy people. Maybe if I had enough daiquiris on River Street beforehand.

[32] I say ish because there are a few that seem to be in flux—New Mexico State's program recently became a victim of budget cuts.

[33] Conspicuously, the University of Kentucky does not have a team in the middle of horse country.

down the road as they're paying equitation bills, but it's better than nothing.

The teams are divided evenly into hunt seat riders and western riders. This is the rare college sport where half of the team doesn't really know what the other half is doing in competition, unlike the whole football team just wondering what a kicker does. The hunt seat riders compete in the usual over fences equitation and a flat equitation, which is similar to dressage and unlike any of the normal flat classes of show jumping. The western riders compete in reining, which involves lots of spinning around, stopping, sliding and cowboy hats. They also do horsemanship, which is a kind of dressage for western riders.[34] The hunt seat riders usually come from the A-circuit, with local riders occasionally walking on to the teams. Unless you've won an equitation final, you recruit yourself by sending in riding videos to the coaches. Equitation competition is commonly mandatory for evaluation purposes. During riders' senior years of high school, their social media accounts will be littered with recruiting visit pictures on the field at big football games before they eventually decide on their college of choice. Then fall comes and they post pictures of the mountains of free sports gear they get as a Division 1 athlete. This is the coolest until you see the pictures from other girls flying private back to their Ivy after hearing them talk about how difficult their training schedule is at the Grand Prix press conference.

In the competition, each team chooses five riders to compete in each of the four phases. What makes the college

---

[34] I greatly apologize to any horsemanship competitors for grossly oversimplifying your sport that I have no intention of understanding. You keep horsemanshipping.

equitation unique is that competitors ride horses provided by the home team's barn, then a rider from the other team rides the same horse and whoever gets the higher score from the judge gets a point for their team. This theoretically makes the competition more equal as the horse's ability affects both riders equally. There are still some built-in advantages. The riders from the home team are using horses they practice on, so they have a greater knowledge of them. Also, the order in which the riders go may be an advantage given that horse's temperament, and, going second may give the rider a chance to glean information from the first round as well as an idea of what kind of score they need to win. The orders and horses are randomly drawn, so it is still made to be as fair as possible. I immediately recognized this format from my days playing duplicate bridge in college, where your team plays a hand of cards then the other team plays the same hand and whoever attains a better result wins. While our bidding conventions were tested, the variable of a live animal (other than our own animalistic natures) was not in play for us at the Collegiate Bridge Championships.[35] The horses they use are owned by the school and are usually donated, so they vary in quality. The top schools have some nice ones donated from professionals which are almost always used for the meets. Occasionally, accomplished equitation riders will arrive and have difficulty adjusting to not being able to only compete on top horses, but for the most part riders are there because of their riding ability and not their horse's ability. During a meet, a western phase and a hunt seat phase will compete simultaneously, then there will be a halftime and the other

---

[35] I try not to bring up my bridge skills at horse shows because of the hoard of ladies that it would attract.

two phases will again compete simultaneously.[36] They usually have the reining go with the equitation flat and the over fences go with the horsemanship so at least one exciting class is always under way. The winner of a meet is the team that accumulates the most points over the 20 head-to-head match ups.

This competition produces a very interesting team dynamic, as only a maximum of 20 people on the team are "show girls," or competitors during the meets with other schools. On the hunt seat side, some riders do both of the competitions, so there can be anywhere from 5-10 show girls for the two events and they do not change from meet to meet. Most of the NCEA teams have 30-40 riders, but Georgia and Baylor have around 70. So, at any given time, anywhere from half to a fourth of the team is actually competing. The rest are far from benchwarmers as they all have duties on meet days. The home team is required to supply a warm up rider for each horse, who is responsible for riding during a warm up period before the competition. This is to give the riders from both teams a chance to evaluate the horse they've drawn before they ride it in the competition. This occupies at least 10 riders during each round, with up to 20 if no one does it twice at a meet. The rest of the team has duties such as barn manager, runner, scribe, videographer, and even social media. There is no seniority involved in the assignment of these positions. Riders can arrive and immediately be a show girl or go all four years and not compete in a meet. I can see where it might be somewhat disheartening for a rider that goes from showing

---

[36] This arrangement still blows my mind. It would be like at a tennis match if in half the matches people played badminton. I am not sure that I totally agree with it, but I have not experienced enough college eq in person to formulate a strong opinion.

frequently on the A-circuit to rarely, if ever, competing at the college level, but it seemed that many riders acclimate themselves to the team dynamic and their roles in its success. They still have the opportunity to ride on a regular basis, though not on a competitive level, and can always work towards a goal of being a show girl or doing warm up at the meets.

The season runs from September to April with around 17 meets, but it is less daunting than it appears. They take a break from Thanksgiving until mid-January for finals, and the regular season ends at the beginning of March before conference finals and the national championship in late March and April. Also, some teams only take a smaller amount of riders to the away meets and the championships. A typical practice schedule for a rider includes four 45 minute workouts a week in the gym, which can involve cardio, weightlifting and pilates; and, two hour-long riding lessons a week, with optional "free rides" once a week. The riding lessons are then only limited to the show girls and happen more frequently as the season goes on and only the year-end tournaments remain. It is not the arduous time commitment that a football or basketball athlete might have.

Aside from the structural fairness of its competition, college equestrian team competition is unlike anything else in the sport. Equestrian competition outside of college is by and large an individual sport. You may ride with a barn and cheer on people with whom you train or go to shows, but your success depends on your performance alone. Only in Nations Cup-style competition is there a team-like element. For the most part these are constantly changing groups with other riders from your zone or country. The scoring is still individual, with the rider trying to attain a clear jumping round regardless of what the other team members do. Even the biggest Nations Cup-style events like the Olympics have an individual component that is more prestigious and scored partially from the team scores. At the college level, there are virtually no individual elements of competition. You either get a standardized point for your team or don't, and your team wins or loses. They will award individual accolades like MOP (Most Outstanding Performance) to the highest score of each round and name All-American riders at the end of the year, but the only result that matters is the team's success.[37] In addition, contrary to the impersonal nature of the Nations Cup teams, college team riders practice together, work out together and frequently live together, creating a sorority like environment. This not only creates a level of camaraderie unattainable in any other sort of equestrian competition. It also adds a new level of pressure, as your performance can win or lose a meet for your team.

I was initially skeptical about the nature of college equestrian. That college riders are not guaranteed show participation and team members are required to perform non-riding duties leads me to think that team size is determined as much by the need to fulfill title IX requirements as much if not more than any other factor. It appears to be a way to force unwitting riders who wanted to ride in college to do the equitation classes, or give the riders at the big eq barns a reason to be investing so much time and money. There is some irony in well financed riders from the northeast

---

[37] The MOP winners are usually awarded flowers after meets, making it seem sort of like a beauty pageant. In rare instances, they have sometimes gotten medals or even cake. That's right, cake.

spending large sums of money and time on equitation only to enroll in a large state school in the south on a partial scholarship. It does make sense to parents in that their daughters get to constantly ride and compete without them having to foot any of the related expenses—at least for a few months out of the year. There is some lack of awareness among prospective college team riders as to what is entailed in a college equestrian program. I frequently talked to riders who were being recruited or were headed to a school in the fall who had little idea of what they were getting into or what their chances were of showing on the team. The program is not for everyone, but after learning more I am impressed by its unique contributions to the sport. Imagine if every equitation final was determined by riders having to compete on the same horse, or an Olympic rider was unfazed by the team competition because she had won the determining point for her team at NCEA finals. It would undoubtedly be a positive thing if more elements of collegiate equestrian were present at hunter/jumper shows.

CHAPTER EIGHT

Costs
Turn Back Now

It is now time to discuss the costs associated with horses and showing. These costs are universally and reductively thought of as high. If you are a parent regularly footing the bill for riding, I would not start this chapter before procuring an amber-colored alcohol of your choice to imbibe while reading. If you are a junior rider whose parents foot said bills, this will either make you feel shame or agitation that I have misrepresented the costs of the sport as far too low or high. If you are the sibling of a rider, this will provide sufficient ammunition to combat the perceived monetary inequality your parents exhibit towards between their offspring. If you are totally out of the sport, you may want to protect yourself from injury due to profuse head-shaking.

Even after watching it for a year, I thought I knew riding was expensive and the people who did it were mostly wealthy. As I learned how much it actually cost, I was stunned by how numerous and intricate the expenses were. For example, when you buy a saddle, which runs in the thousands of dollars, you not only have to buy stirrups (the things you hook on it to put your feet in when you ride) for a couple hundred dollars, but you also have to buy the leather bands that attach the stirrups to the saddle for another hundred or more dollars. This sort of exorbitant pricing followed by constant unexpected expenses epitomizes the show jumping finance experience. Horse expenses tend to accrue incrementally as they come from many different places. Instead of getting a huge bill every six months for everything you've spent on the sport, you are spending smaller, slightly less ridiculous sums on a monthly basis.

In my explanation, costs are divided into low end and high end figures. The low end figure represents the minimum someone would spend on something while still competing at A-circuit horse shows. That is, if you have enough money to spend $500 a week showing at higher-end shows, you are likely not going to spend only $50 on an Ovation Helmet when they can get a far superior One K Helmet for $250. So while in many cases there are lower quality or secondhand items available for lower prices than the low end figures that I mention, you will almost never see them at higher level competitions. In most examples you will rarely see many of the low end options at A-circuit shows. Using the helmet example, probably 95% of the riders at the show have a GPA, Charles Owen or Samshield helmet, most of which are over $400 and would constitute the high end figure. I only provide the low end figure to give an idea of what would be a reasonable price for someone that would actually compete at that level. The majority of riders are going to buy the high end equipment or services or something close to it.

I've divided the costs up into four sections: the horse itself and its care and maintenance, the tack or equipment for the horse, the apparel for the rider and showing costs. For all the sections except the rider apparel, it's important to remember that the costs are multiplied by the number of horses you have, and very few A-circuit riders have only one horse. This is either because they have a horse for each of the three specific disciplines in which they compete (hunters, jumpers and equitation), or because they have multiple rides to increase their chances of winning and the number of horses they can train. With a few exceptions, most of the horse-related expenses are not decreased by having multiple horses.

HORSE & CARE

The greatest expense in show jumping is usually the horse you ride. There are two options for horse ownership: owning the horse or leasing it. A horse lease (very different than a car lease) usually works with you paying around one-third of the horse's value yearly, plus the horse's monthly expenses and is commonly for a six or twelve-month basis. The price of a horse depends on many variables: its jumping ability, age, results, owner, and what discipline it competes in. An entire book could be written on the nuances of buying and selling them. A horse's value can fluctuate wildly. To give you a general idea, at a smaller A-circuit show you will see very few horses purchased for or worth under $20,000. Most are purchased for under $250,000, with the median being around $50,000-$75,000. At a big show like WEF, where it costs more money to show and is more competitive, the low end value of the horses entered is $75,000, the median is $250,000-

$350,000 and the high end is $500,000-$650,000. At the upper limit, some top Grand Prix horses will sell for millions of dollars.

I know what you are thinking—these horses cost as much as a house. Or you might be a rider and think I am off in my price ranges. Either way, it is a bit jarring to look into a crowded schooling ring at WEF and realize that you easily could be looking at $10 million in money spent on the horses just in that ring. This is one of the main factors that separates the A-circuit hunter/jumper world from your friend's daughter that did a few local jumper shows as a teenager. It is almost comically expensive and results in a fairly homogenous upper-class rider base, especially at the junior levels. After my year-long immersion, it is easier to question the sanity of riders from a non-upper class background who try to succeed on the A-circuit than to question their ambition. The second point regarding the value of horses is that prices are the way they are because the market sets them. These horses' intrinsic value is probably nowhere near their purchase price. Very few horses will make more money than they are worth, especially factoring in their care and show costs. The price is inflated because the buyer base has a large amount of capital and the correlation between the quantity and quality of horses available and your chances to succeed in the sport.

Now that you have likely sunk more than the per-capita GDP of most of the world on your furry new equine friend, you get to pay for its upkeep. It is tempting to compare a horse to some other expensive, low return-on-value purchase like a boat, where you spend a lot of money on it for the privilege to spend more maintaining it, but this would diminish the horse's needs as a living, breathing creature.

Hunter/jumper horses are some of the best cared for animals in the world. Little expense is spared in their care because of their high worth, the wealth of their owners and because of how it can directly affect their performance in the ring. They have everything: horse chiropractors, horse treadmills, horse treading pools. The main care expense that all horses have is board. A-circuit horses do not go back home and stay in their owners' backyards. Most stay at a full-service training barn with riding rings, where they also receive instruction. Some of these barns have a second location in Wellington for the winter. Board price can vary wildly based on location and the services offered, but you should expect to pay at least $800 a month for a decent barn situation no matter your location. It is more common for it to be above $1,000 a month, and in Wellington the price increases even more during the winter season. The top equitation barns are known to charge upwards of $3,500 a month for board, not including training fees at shows. This is the point where the evaporating money starts to eat at me. With a horse's price, you could almost talk yourself into the purchase as an investment, as there is some small chance you could sell it for as much or more than you paid for it. Board is just money flying out the window, never to be seen again. Even though it's necessary, if I had a horse I would still make someone else write the checks to retain what might be left of my sanity.

Once you have a home for a horse, you are inundated with an avalanche of other financial responsibilities before you even think about getting on your horse. Feed can cost anywhere from $50-$300 a month. Most take supplements, which adds another few hundred. They need to have their feet done by a farrier once a month, at a cost of around $200-

$400.[38] Most horses have insurance, which could easily stretch into five figures a year for a valuable horse. Vet costs can skyrocket if anything happens, but even routine shots and check-ups can cost around $1,500 a year. A trainer told me you should easily expect to spend around $8,000 to $10,000 just on annual maintenance costs. This doesn't include board—with it we are already at around $24,000 a year, plus whatever you initially paid for the horse and we haven't ridden yet. I feel like I'm about to pass out.

HORSE TACK

I've always found tack to be a fun word for horse gear. It is apparently an abbreviation of "tackle" as you might say "fishing tackle." Maybe someone decided once football was invented that we wouldn't want to suggest knocking horses to the ground when discussing bridles. Also, most tack is leather, which can have a tacky feel to it. Horse tack is generally not cheap, and there is an abundance of it. With the exception of maybe a saddle, very little tack is regularly shared by multiple horses. The most expensive item in horse tack is the saddle, so try to take comfort in the fact that you might not need one per horse when you are spending the down payment of a car on it. There are used saddles and a variety of brands of varying quality, but at an A-circuit show most of the saddles you see cost $2,000, while higher end ones can go for $8,000 and up.[39] This price only purchases

---

[38] After finding this out I immediately considered becoming a farrier before realizing that I can't be within a football field's length of the horrible smell of burning hoof. Give me manure over burning hoof any day.

[39] Again, I have no idea how hard it is to be a saddler but am I now definitely considering it. The smell would actually be a plus in this case.

you the saddle. Additional purchases are required for the stirrups ($195-$300), and even the leather that connects the stirrups to the saddle ($100-$190). And you can't just put a saddle on a horse—you need to put a saddle pad ($30-$65) on first, followed by a halfpad ($170-$250), with both sides of it connected by a girth ($90-$450) underneath the horse to hold it in place. So for anywhere from $2,600-$9,300, you can now sit on your horse.

You will now need the equipment to allow you to control your horse. This includes a bridle ($250-$650) that goes around its head and two attachments, a bit or metal mouthpiece ($25-$725) and reins ($75-$325) that the rider holds. From here, there is a variety of optional but common training tools: a martingale ($70-$425), which attaches the bridle to the girth and keeps the horse from raising its head too high, boots ($80-$700), which go on the horses' legs above their hooves and protect them from contact with objects when jumping; and a myriad of other accessories that can add up—draw reins, lunge lines, bell boots, polo wraps, a hackamore. Once you're done riding, you'll need a halter (usually personalized, $40-$120) to lead it around, fly masks, blankets, and even a special shipping halter ($100-$325), if you're planning to trailer your horse anywhere. Now that you have all this great horse tack, you will also need supplies to clean and take care of it as well, including a tack trunk to store it in. I don't think I've ever seen a plastic one; the wooden trunks start around $800 and most are personalized and easily worth over $1,000. At the low end, you will likely spend around $4,200 on horse tack, while most are spending closer to the $14,000 high end mark. Not to mention quite a bit of it will need to be replaced over time. Now, we're ready to go, right? Oh, wait, you're wearing that?

RIDER APPAREL

This is the fun part—shopping for clothes. I secretly believe that part of the popularity of the equestrian world is the shopping for riding apparel needed for competition. There is necessary equipment for riding and a certain outfit is required to compete in most classes. In addition, you need several of each item. You can't very well expect to show three days in a row with only one show shirt and pair of breeches without getting some looks in the schooling ring ranging from disgust to pity. Starting with the necessary and expensive: a helmet ($200-$500, 1-2 quantity) and boots ($400-$2,000, 1-2 pairs). Boots are particularly expensive because they can be custom-fitted to the rider and made from Italian leather. With most of the other apparel, the sums needed can spiral out of control based on the color options (you need white breeches for classic and Grand Prix competition, but tan for normal) and having a separate set of clothing for schooling and showing. The big ticket item in this group is a show jacket ($200-$1,000), sort of an athletic version of a dress blazer which can also be custom tailored. Most riders have two or more of them, and as previously mentioned, female hunter riders are even required to have a shadbelly for derby competitions.[40] You will also need show shirts ($75-$200, 3+), sun shirts ($65-$125, 3+) that are more for schooling, breeches ($100-$400, 3+ show, 3+ schooling), gloves ($20-$85, 2+), spurs

---

[40] To terribly paraphrase Jeff Foxworthy, if something about horses doesn't make sense, then you might be talking about hunters.

($25-$125) and other miscellaneous things like special socks, hairnets, and even special underwear that reduces VPL when wearing breeches. I think the moment I lost my horse show boyfriend innocence was when I learned what VPL was— Visible Panty Lines. You also need a belt, which can be like most any other belt and range from $25-$400, but I frequently see the classic Hermès H belt at the show, yours for only $1,300. It is difficult to determine just how much is regularly spent on apparel because of how much of it you could theoretically buy and the crazy upward options like a Hermès belt. But let's just say for the minimally stocked closet, most A-circuit riders will be spending at least $3,000. If you picked a random rider out of the show ring at WEF, they would likely be wearing the high end selections of all of these items (who wants to skimp when it comes to fashion), with the cost of their complete outfit approaching $7,500. But hey, at least you look good—though you have just paid an exorbitant sum to show up to an event wearing the same outfit as everyone else.

SHOWING

The whole point of this exercise in financial evaporation is to actually compete at an A-circuit show. There are a few eccentric folks who own expensive horses but don't have interest in showing them, but most people don't spend the money on such horses without competing at this level. You may be shocked to discover that the costs involved with showing on the hunter/jumper A-circuit are abundant and high. Some shows are less expensive to show at than others, but not by a wide margin based on show fees. The basic costs associated with showing are found on the show bill, which reads like a Ticketmaster receipt on steroids—tons of random nickel-and-dime charges. You pay a basic entry fee for every class you compete in with your horse, the scale of which is determined by whether or not there is prize money in a class. For classes with no prize money, expect to pay around $45— for prize money, it is generally around 5-10% of the purse for lower prize money classes and 1-2% for ones above $25,000. You then also have to pay for a stall if you are keeping your horse on the premises for the show week (~$250+) or trailering or bringing it in from off-site (~$50). This is where things start getting a bit fee-crazy. Per horse, there is an office fee, ambulance fee, USEF fee, USHJA zone fee and nighttime security fee, all of which adds up to around $100-$125. Then, there is the craziest of fees, something I only learned about when my girlfriend was finally showing almost two years into my horse show odyssey—the nomination fee. I learned about this because I wanted to encourage her to compete in a class with more prize money so we might actually offset some of the show costs. You see, if your horse competes in jumper classes with non-negligible prize money (purses over $500), there is a nomination fee cost to participate in them that ranges from $175-$250. This fee is ostensibly to cover the prize money purse for the class... but shouldn't the entry fee do that? I have seen no evidence to the contrary that this fee is anything more than profit for the event. A show bill alone can run at least $500 per horse and more commonly around $800 and up per show.

With the show bill taken care of, the real showing expenses begin. If you ride with a trainer, which most juniors do, you have to pay for that trainer's time and sometimes even lodging at the show split with their other clients. Training arrangements vary greatly. Some trainers' fees are included in the board of the horse while top equitation trainers charge thousands of dollars per show. Most riders have at least one groom tending to their horses at the show. They run about $100 a day depending on skill and experience. Unless you own a trailer and a pickup truck, you also likely have to pay to ship your horse to and from the show, which can cost hundreds of dollars depending on the distance. You also are responsible for your own lodging and transportation to and from the show. At WEF, a large portion of the juniors fly in from the northeast for the weekend while also renting expensive housing for the three-month period. This section has many more intangibles because of the variety of showing situations you can be in, so quantifying a total yearly cost of showing is difficult. Most top A-circuit riders will show over half of the twelve weeks at WEF, do three to four shows in April and May, around six or seven until late September before the four or five indoors shows, totaling anywhere from 18 to 32 or more show weeks a year. While many less active riders will likely spend in the low five figures, it is easy for an active A-circuit rider to spend up to $100,000 per horse per year on show costs.

SUMMARY

In some ways, the layout of expenses offered above still does not provide the complete accounting picture that you might see in an audit of an A-circuit rider. There are other things to spend money on, both necessary and not, in addition to what I have mentioned. For example, to compete at some specialty shows I attended such as Miami and Central Park, you might be required to purchase a VIP table for the duration of the event that costs five figures. Some riders also purchase VIP tables at most of the events they compete in, simply because they can. In my experience, what I thought I knew about how costly the sport was—the publicized price of top-dollar horses and how wealthy everyone seemed to be that competed was the tip of the iceberg. There are more ways to spend money than you can imagine.

In laying out the above expenses, I want to reiterate in a way that I would normally put in all caps if I were writing like a television pundit: this is per horse, and most people have multiple horses. You must suspend disbelief in this alternate reality when you are talking to the lovely girl at WEF with two junior hunters and an eq horse and not think about the fact that she likely spent $500,000 on her horses, $26,000 to outfit them with tack, $72,000 a year to care for them and $300,000 a year to show them in $7,500 worth of clothing she wears specifically to ride. This is a family-friendly book, but I need to depart from that for one moment: holy shit. Therein lies the terrible beauty of how expensive the sport is. Its expenses are so multifaceted and fragmented that you can avoid the harsh realities of the true bottom line. You know it's expensive, but until some dilettante like me writes a chapter like this and adds it all up, you can ignore the fact that it's perfectly reasonable for a large percentage of participants in a sport to spend a half a million dollars initially and then again every year on it.

PART 2

The Shows

CHAPTER NINE

Wellington

I Saw Beezie at Publix

When I first moved to West Palm Beach, I quickly became aware of the stark division between my new residence and one of the most wealthy enclaves in the US, Palm Beach. The huge mansions were difficult to miss, just across the water from downtown. I wondered, who were these people? How had they accumulated this wealth? And why did they choose to be here, on this ridiculously priced real estate? Unbeknownst to me, just as close to my new apartment was an area just as exclusive and expensive. Palm Beach was easy to spot, Wellington wasn't. My girlfriend had showed as a junior in Wellington, back when it held smaller events and was more of a low-key horse community. Shortly after our arrival we went exploring, trying to find where she used to show on a quiet Sunday summer evening. We got lost around back roads that led to expansive polo fields and paddocks flanked by large palms, seeing roads familiar to her but not the grounds themselves. Eventually we gave up and headed home. The closest I came to understanding that I was on the periphery of the center of the horse show world was the city welcome signs having a horse head actually intertwined into the word "Wellington." A half a year would pass before the masses would descend on the area, their gravity pulling me in to this new and unfamiliar horse show world.

But, at some point in the not-so-distant past, it was all swamp. It's easy to imagine, just drive a few miles west or south and civilization will abruptly cease to exist as the edges of the swampy Everglades greet you. Why here? Maybe its proximity to Palm Beach? The swamp could have become many things, but only the quirks of the hunter/jumper world could have transformed it into Wellington, Florida, where just a mile from the wilderness empty lots sell for millions of dollars because of their proximity to the grounds of the biggest horse show in this hemisphere, the Winter Equestrian Festival.

Unlike some storied European showjumping epicenter, Wellington has the short history you would expect from a former swamp. In 1951, an accountant from New England named Charles Oliver Wellington bought most of the land that today bears his name. He named his land "Flying Cow Ranch;" flying because he was an aviator, Cow because these were his initials.[41] Other than this, there is little evidence to suggest he did anything other than lend his respectable English surname to the project. He died 8 years after purchasing the land without a clue that one day very wealthy teenage girls would be standing on it, sipping Starbucks and talking about how pushy CWD sales reps are while waiting for their flat class. Another central figure in Wellington's history is the local agent who sold Wellington the land,

---

[41] Some people may find this name still relevant today when they are watching hunter rounds.

Arthur "Bink" Glisson. Glisson maintained Wellington's land for him as it was drained and leveed to make it suitable farmland. The "Binks Forest" name is now on an elementary school and country club in town.

Development of the land officially started in the 1970s. Included with the residential subdivisions and golf complexes was a polo and country club, probably to cater to the Palm Beach crowd. It took only a few years for the equestrian community to coalesce in the area, first around polo by hosting the Polo World Cup, then around show jumping with the Winter Equestrian Festival, where they held the Olympic trials for show jumping. Throughout the late '80s and '90s, it remained a winter refuge on the hunter/jumper circuit, but resembled many of the other shows today as a sort of ramshackle showgrounds with a simple grass ring, port-a-potties and little spectator seating. It was not exactly thriving, but it was a serviceable place for people to compete. Its rise to its current level started around the time of its purchase by Mark Bellissimo in 2006. While I have little personal grasp of the climate of the show jumping scene ten years ago, it seems that Bellissimo took over WEF as the sport was expanding to what it is today. He fostered this at WEF by adding competition rings, including a main arena and VIP section, and essentially making a showground that could serve as the epicenter of competition for North America as the sport grew. WEF today is a gargantuan affair, with 12 main show weeks spanning January to April, a Pre-Circuit in November and December and smaller shows year-round. There are few other, if any, shows that offer as much top-level competition and prize money in a consecutive week series. It is also one of the most-attended shows, with thousands of entries weekly. WEF has the additional benefit of it being, aside from smaller shows in Ocala and in California, the only option for high-level hunter/jumper competition during the winter months. WEF has become a juggernaut that cannot be ignored on any North American junior or professional's schedule, and as such, is unlike any other show I visited. WEF's culture is essentially a microcosm of the show jumping culture because it concentrates in a small area for almost a third of the year.

I had no idea that any of this was going on so close to me in West Palm Beach, and really the only way any nearby resident would experience it first hand is if they were at Dunkin' Donuts in Wellington and happened to see two girls on horseback in the drive-thru. Above all, I didn't see what the big deal was. It was sort of like growing up in North Carolina and just willfully choosing to ignore all the NASCAR around me. There were horses, people rode on them, so what? My girlfriend wasn't a Jeff Gordon fan, but she was a fan of Margie Engle. She started going to WEF during its first few weeks in January and taking pictures, and I finally acquiesced and agreed to meet her out there one Sunday. When you get close to the show, you realize how equestrian-centered the community of Wellington is when you see there are horse paths instead of sidewalks and horses crossing major intersections. Upon arrival to the showgrounds, I had no idea how badly I would need a map. The layout is vast and makes little sense. Some rings are numbered, some have generic names like "Rost" or "Grand Hunter" and quite a few are identical looking. As I walked in to meet my girlfriend, she told me she was at the "DeNemethy" ring, so I looked at the map from the entrance and started what I assumed to be the quickest path to it around the outside of the main stadium ring. Unfortunately, I did not realize I had chosen the side where there are no other rings and is used as a service entrance for the catering in the VIP section. I soon found myself on a narrow strip of road surrounded by haphazard jump material and mopeds and golf carts whizzing by. Eventually I found my way to the wrong side of the ring, but it was not the glorious introduction to the Palm Beach International Equestrian Center that one might anticipate.

I sat on some uncomfortable wooden levels next to the ring with a smattering of other spectators and watched horses jump over very high jumps with ease. About ten minutes in, I suddenly felt like Neo standing in front of Morpheus offering me the blue pill or the red pill. I could continue to remain blissfully ignorant about the horse show world except what managed to come in through osmosis and my life would go on as normal. Or, I could start peppering my girlfriend with questions trying to understand it and see how deep the rabbit hole goes. Most people I've met in my position seem to take the red pill, which I can understand. It can be difficult to become fully interested in something you know nothing about, even if it is something someone you care about does.[42] For some strange reason I took the blue pill and began asking questions, and ultimately felt the need to write a book to justify it all. I would encourage those who heartily accepted the other option to reconsider, as it is a vast and interesting world behind the banal, repetitive equine gymnastics.

I quizzed my girlfriend constantly about matters big and small as I was shown around the sprawling showgrounds. "Why is there a ring next to the one with the jumps with a bunch of horses?" (A schooling ring where one warms up)

---

[42] Just ask everyone whose best friends think they race horses.

"How do you win?" (see The Basics chapter) and "Who buys all this crap?" I was referring to how seemingly every inch of possible real estate is covered with vendors peddling their wares, mostly in tiny white tents. This gave it a sort of "refugee camp for millionaires" feel. Palm Beach International Equestrian Center, or PBIEC, is not a rustic showground by any means, but it has a surprising lack of permanent structures and general opulence given WEF's size and prestige. Most who stable their horses on-site will pay handsomely for unimpressive tent stalls. I am not privy to the political situation in the area but I believe it has something to do with stymying the development. I will say that I never had to use a port-a-potty on site, as they had a number of nice bathrooms in buildings and one or two large, trailer-sized portable bathrooms. I had never been in one of these contraptions before, and as I walked up the steps and into the much-less-used men's side, I was greeted with air-conditioning, hardwood flooring and cabinets and faux-marble walls. Above the three urinals was a framed photo of a golf swing progressing. It was then I began to understand I was in a different kind of place.[43]

I would eventually return again and again after my first visit and began to learn the lay of the land. The only off limits location other than the insides of the rings themselves was a large covered area, or International Club, next to the main stadium, or International Ring. This is a VIP area where you purchase a table and during show days are provided with food and drinks. It costs at minimum five figures for the 12 weeks,

---

[43] I would end up snapping a picture of these urinals and using it as the profile picture for my Horse Show Boyfriend Twitter account, as if to prove my name.

and they are always booked to capacity for the circuit. For the vast majority participating at WEF, this is a small drop in the bucket for their overall equestrian expenses and wealth. This is why vendors pay over five figures for the duration of the circuit and populate the majority of the pedestrian areas of the showgrounds in their tiny tents. The International Arena holds the highest level competition throughout the show and it is something of a milestone to show there for a rider. On the end where competitors enter from the schooling ring, they go underneath a large green pedestrian bridge bearing the name of the venue. This is a must-have backdrop for any good jumping photo. Certain outside rings also hold the big equitation and hunter events, and there are even two rings split off from the main cluster where pony competition is held. This is referred to as "Pony Island" and there have even been hats with the name and a skull and crossbones made for that section of the showgrounds. Occasionally, competition overflows to their other venue across the street, the Global Dressage Festival grounds, where there is a smaller stadium and a few rings along with a large grass derby field. I attended major dressage competition there once or twice on a Friday night, and I would tell you more but I blocked out as much of it as I could.[44]

On Saturday nights during WEF, "Saturday Night Lights" are held, where they have big Grand Prix or specialty events in the packed International Arena. They most recently held the US Olympic Trials in Wellington but have since done away with the event in the interest of not overworking the horses.

---

[44] My main memories are of Charlotte Jorst and Laura Graves and that every dressage rider looks like they won the lottery after they finish a round.

There is the usual big Nations Cup event and multiple 5* FEI Grand Prix events, but the specialty events also include the Battle of the Sexes and the Great Charity Challenge. Battle of the Sexes, usually held in one of the first weeks, is an event where 8-10 professional male riders compete against 8-10 professional female riders in a series of unusual events like a relay and a head-to-head race. The head-to-head race is amazing to watch, as the two riders do a shortened identical course at the same time and pass through the timers side-by-side racing style. The jumps aren't huge, but there is a competitive element that is very crowd-pleasing. The Great Charity Challenge is an event a few weeks into the circuit where teams of three riders, usually two amateurs and one professional, compete to win money for a local charity. Everyone also dresses up based on a yearly theme, such as superheroes or fairy tales. The competition is secondary to the hilarious costumes that some riders wear. It is so popular to compete in that you will often see multiple iterations of Shrek or Frozen depending on that year's theme. The riders and sponsors pay a steep fee for the opportunity to dress up and compete, and the money in turn goes to selected local charities. My first Great Charity Challenge experience occurred in the rain, which made it even more amusing to watch. These events also serve to break up what can be a very large and expensive grind of a show schedule for the participating riders.

The general itinerary for a WEF show week for junior riders begins when most fly in Thursday evening from New England or wherever else they live. They then wake up at 5am on Friday, Saturday and Sunday and compete in numerous equitation, jumper or hunter classes under the tutelage of their big name trainer before jetting off Sunday evening. This is repeated 6-10 times more during the winter. It is a grueling and costly schedule for these weekend snowbirds, with plane tickets and lodging expenses adding to the already steep show bill—of which WEF has maybe the most expensive on circuit. Wellington has hardly any hotels, save for one basic Hampton Inn that is known to charge up to $300 a night during circuit. Since WEF is a mandatory event for junior riders pursuing equitation finals or any high-level success, all have to find a lodging solution in the area. WEF is where judges learn who you are, trainers recognize and foster talent and where riders catch ride, or ride horses of other owners eager to show them off. Riders either grow up spending every winter there or aspire to one day attend, only to realize that they have spent a small fortune to compete in a 75 entry class with long odds of winning. This is, of course, the cynical horse show boyfriend view who doesn't experience the magic of showing at Wellington. At the base level, people show horses to be seen riding them (hence the verb "show"), and there is no place where more eyes are on you and your results than at WEF. The other fun part of showing at WEF for riders is the possibility to actually beat the long odds and win an ultra-competitive class. Even placing is exciting, but winning at WEF beats winning anywhere else on the A-circuit. Once the showing is done, WEF has more social media posting opportunities than any other show. Everyone has to know about your walks through the trail to Grand Prix village, your barn trail rides and even your soufflés at Echo after it's over. And because it goes on for three months, the fun doesn't have to stop on Sunday night or Monday as you pack up and go on to another show.

When professionals ride in the ring, they are announced along with their horse and where their operation is based. More often than not, you will hear "based out of Wellington, FL" because in their nomadic life, Wellington is where they spend the most amount of time. While setting up shop in Wellington makes logistical sense, it is not cheap. Palatial barns that are a few minutes' ride from the showgrounds can cost tens of millions of dollars. Two exclusive neighborhoods adjacent to the grounds are Grand Prix Village and Mallet Hill. Anyone with a barn in these neighborhoods will have substantial financial resources.[45] The surrounding areas also have great value and rent will be accordingly expensive. If you are getting a reasonable price on a stall or barn rental during the circuit, there is likely something wrong with it or it is actually under construction. Staying in these permanent facilities for three months allows riders time to either find a new horse from a large selection in the area or develop a relationship with a current horse by keeping their environment stable.

The only thing more extreme than Wellington property values and rent are the partying habits of equestrians, including both professional and junior/amateur (with fake ID). I suppose being awake all day and adopting a daredevil mindset that allows you to jump over four foot fences with ease breeds a certain desire to get krunk when the workday is over. The main watering holes are The Player's Club, or just "Players" and The Grille, both of which are upscale dining establishments that transform into club-like atmospheres

---

[45] At press an empty 9-acre lot in Mallet Hill was selling for $14 million. I would say something funny here but I'm too busy googling "how to be a real estate agent in Wellington."

after hours. I have never been to either because I am actually a 75-year-old, so I can't report back on the debauchery that goes on there. I can say that Wellington has more than its share of DUIs by riders. Wealthy people seem to have some aversion to using their financial means for drivers when they have been drinking. Another strange twist to the Wellington party scene is that the big night out is Sunday, as it is the end of the show week and Mondays are days off. WEF also encourages the party scene to a degree by turning one of the buildings next to the main ring into a club-like atmosphere after the Saturday Night Lights competition, which draws quite a few locals who would not otherwise be at a horse show.

The main engine of Wellington's success is its concentration of top talent. For three months out of the year, it becomes the center for hunter/jumper equestrian competition unlike any other show on the circuit. The itinerant horse show lifestyle calms, and there is a concentration of everyone on the same odd riding and showing routine. You can't go to a restaurant or grocery store in town without seeing someone in breeches. It's almost like a camp for horse show people, where they actually have time to have fun with people living the same bizarre lifestyle. I would only realize how unique this is about WEF when I ventured to the other, smaller shows. Instead of sticking a toe into the horse show kiddie pool, I had cannonballed directly into a deep, blue-dyed water jump.

CHAPTER TEN

Old Salem

Through the Woods to Grandmother's House

The visit to Old Salem started auspiciously by going through the town of Fishkill, NY. I had very little idea of what to expect at my first horse show other than WEF and in my first trip to the state of New York. My visit ended up being confined to a small section of the state north of NYC in the Poughkeepsie/Danbury, CT area that serves as a retreat for wealthy New Yorkers. It was only after attending many other horse shows that I developed some perspective on the uniqueness of Old Salem, a two-week show based at a show barn in North Salem, NY that takes place in May.

North Salem is a community much like many of the others I visited—affluent with a rich tradition of fox-hunting. The two are not mutually exclusive. I don't imagine lower to middle class folks back in the 50s donning the red jackets and taking their hunters through the brush as a weekend activity. In a 1996 New York Times piece about the fox-hunting scene in North Salem, they noted that the prey had grown to include coyotes and that most hunts were accompanied by a "sandwich box and flask." This is the only evidence I have found thus far of the appeal of fox-hunting.

Old Salem Farm's history is a bit more interesting: it was initially built in 1964 by four retired policemen who knew little of what they were doing. However, they were smart enough to enlist the help of a young hunter/jumper rider who had just turned professional—George Morris. George spent a year there using it as his stable, and was the first of many illustrious equestrians to spend time there. It apparently was not initially profitable and changed ownership many times over the next 20 years before falling into the hands of Paul Newman in 1981 (whose daughters rode). The farm was later sold in 1984 to Paul Greenwood, who was a hedge-fund manager who spent lavishly on renovations.[46] It would later be bought by the current owners of Old Salem at a deeply discounted price at auction. The current year-round trainer at the barn is equitation trainer Frank Madden, a brother of the John/Beezie Madden equestrian royalty. Frank moved to Old Salem some years after leaving the equitation powerhouse Beacon Hill, which he ran with his wife Stacia Madden.

Today, Old Salem is one of the shows scattered along the East Coast that riders go to more for its history and location rather than for the prize money. Many top riders have barn operations nearby and it is, along with the Hampton Classic, one of the few shows that all riders from New England inevitably enter. For the less serious junior and amateur riders, Old Salem and the Hampton Classic are like the Easter and Christmas of the hunter/jumper A-circuit. Riders from NYC and the vicinity often have their high-powered

---

[46] After selling the farm in 2001, Greenwood was convicted in 2009 of securities fraud in excess of $600 million. That's a lot of ornate stall guards.

bankrolling parents attend the Old Salem Show. A trip down to Wellington is a bit much for the Michael Bloombergs and Jerry Seinfelds of the world, but an hour drive up to Westchester County leaves little excuse for them not to watch their progeny. Old Salem Farm also currently hosts another show in the fall, the American Gold Cup, which is a more prestigious FEI sanctioned show.

As a showgrounds Old Salem is opulent, but still a barn. It has an expansive grass derby field, two other rings with footing and a small indoor arena. The derby field is the crown jewel and is the recognizable feature of the show. It is sprawling, charmingly uneven, and has a few large natural elements such as trees and water. Old Salem has the luxury of being in use as a show only 3 or so weeks a year, so its field is generally pristine. Two aspects involving cars dulled the magic for me. The main entrance road is on the other side of the showgrounds such that, you not only lose one side of seating but you see cars speeding by while watching the rounds. The second distraction was something I soon realized was a common element of shows—there were a bevy of luxury cars parked throughout the ring. To me, the presence of large amounts of horsepower detracted from the bucolic scenery. The juxtaposition of the premium motor cars with horses easily worth 5 to 10 times as the cars as them was interesting, though.[47]

For spectators, there are metal bleachers set up around the derby field and one of the other rings, but the hunter ring basically has no seating other than a fence atop a hill that overlooks one side of the ring. Now is when I could make a

---

[47] The only incident I heard about with cars in the ring was that applause caused a dressage horse to spook in to a Land Rover and put a dent in it.

joke about no one wanting to watch hunters anyway, but I'm sure whatever grandparent came in for the day probably didn't find it funny when they had nowhere to sit and watch the small children's hunters. Perhaps the best amenity of the facility was a very nice lounge area on the 2nd floor of the barn that overlooked the indoor arena. There was plush leather furniture and candy available at one of the "do high school at home because you ride horses" programs' designated "study area." I spent quite a bit of time hiding out up here attempting to get a cell signal, and I can attest that I never saw one person studying. I did eat a lot of the candy though.

Speaking of sweets, one of the other Old Salem traditions I enjoyed was a free Ben & Jerry's ice cream social on Saturday. There weren't a variety of flavors and they served it in infinitesimally small cups, but it was free Ben & Jerry's nonetheless. Aside from this, the food selection for non-VIP members (of which there were few) was limited to a carnival-esque trailer feeding you things you shouldn't be eating multiple times a week. I could almost feel the VIPs' amusement at me getting fat from the enormous two story VIP structure on the far side of the grass ring. There was a very nice bar area overlooking another side of the ring where I spent a good deal of time when I wasn't enjoying the lounge.

Old Salem also had an impressive concentration of vendors peddling their wares to the well-heeled attendees. Almost every path from one ring to another was lined with white tents and opportunities to buy. One of the funniest reminders that this facility was still a show barn was that some unfortunate horse had its stall window directly in the middle of an opening in vendor tents situated in front of the main building. He apparently got enough attention that a makeshift sign materialized below him during the show week that said "PLEASE DO NOT PET ME THANK YOU"

Old Salem's other quirks included its accommodation options. I stayed in an Airbnb about 30 minutes away near Fishkill, NY, but the only hotel options were 3 star chains in Danbury, CT. When asked where they were staying, most riders responded "with my grandparents, they have a house near here." I guess technically I was staying at someone's grandmother's house too at my Airbnb.

An amusing twist to Old Salem is that it is scheduled right in the thick of prom season for many of these high school age riders. They are thus presented with the unenviable dilemma of whether to go to this seminal moment in their teenage years or risk upsetting their equitation trainer by skipping a week of showing. I didn't understand how you couldn't just go to prom then wake up early for the eq classes the next morning, but I suppose trying to do the Medal hungover with layers of makeup still on you probably isn't the best look.[48]

One item on the show schedule that caught my eye was the Canine Puissance. Leave it to a horse show to come up with the most highfalutin way to label a height-based jumping competition: Puissance. There are horse Puissances at some shows (Washington being one of the most notable) where the horses take turns making ridiculous 6 to 7 foot leaps over ever-increasing jumps with their fearless riders. This canine version lacked the spellbinding majesty of those. It was basically just a couple of PVC pipes set off to the side of the

---

[48] TJ O'Mara, one of the few males at the big eq barns, told me he opted to skip his prom in favor of the eq classes. That's dedication. Or just not wanting to go to prom.

show ring with dogs running around. They did give out prize money and have winners for each dog size, but it seemed few people were interested in seeing dogs pop up over tiny jumps when they could watch horses go over large ones nearby.

After hearing all this, you may be surprised that there was, in fact, an actual competition of horses jumping and not just an excuse for us all to get together to eat free Ben and Jerry's and avoid prom. Despite being more of a locally attended show, the competition level was very high because many top riders in the US are concentrated in New England. In addition, many of the top equitation barns are also in the area, so they are forced to go against each other in ultra-competitive classes before purposefully splitting up to separate events in the summer. With this in mind (and perhaps because the show is held at an equitation barn of its own), they offered a unique Equitation Challenge event that differed from the normal set at most shows by offering prize money and using a scoring system that included course times. This would have been an inspired idea had they not held it late Saturday afternoon, after riders had already been subjected to a full day of showing that included two other equitation classes that morning (and one the following day). Suddenly a unique competition felt more like a way for eq trainers to encourage their clients to have multiple equitation horses to handle the rigor of a challenging schedule. Not surprisingly, Tori Colvin won as dusk fell.

The next morning, I experienced my first nuanced viewing of classic rounds, usually held on Sunday.[49] In jumper

---

[49] I don't mention the Grand Prix that happened that Sunday afternoon because I was more into watching junior competition at the time, but McLain won like he usually does at Old Salem. No word on if he said "no one comes into my house and beats the king" in the press conference after.

divisions, specific divisions are held numerous times throughout the weekend, usually once per day, with the final round being a classic round where prize money is at stake. Your performance in these previous rounds has no bearing on the final day and they are more warm-up rounds for the bigger event. One of my favorite quirks of classic rounds is that all riders wear white breeches (instead of the usual tan). There are rules that suggest this in the hunter ring for big classes, but it is generally just understood and widely followed in the jumper ring for classic and Grand Prix classes. I have no idea where this originated, but find it amusing that there is an unspoken fashion rule for higher competition.[50] This classic took place on the grass field before the derby, and I had a perfect spot to watch from the aforementioned overlooking bar. In the Medium Jr/AO class, I was treated to my first Tori Colvin jump-off experience. She came in the ring last on Don Juan and proceeded to eviscerate the course with a series of sliced jumps and sharp inside turns after landing, all while going at maximum speed. Having watched enough at that point to know that it was a noticeably different performance than other rides, it reminded me of being back in college at Davidson and watching Steph Curry play. Not his shooting, but his passing—seeing angles that seemingly weren't there before they even existed. A jump-off quickly became my favorite part of the sport that day, not just because of the excitement involved, but because of the execution. Most winners on this shortened course are decided by fractions of a second, so every inch of the course must be planned to perfection. For me, it is still thrilling to see these skilled

---

[50] I'm still waiting to see my first "On Sundays, we wear white" T-shirt.

riders like Tori flawlessly execute their plans, choosing all of the highest degree of difficulty decisions to win.

Tori was back in the High Jr/AO class and had another mind-blowing jump-off round which featured a gasp-inducing gallop to the final jump, over which she soared at just the right moment with one hand on the reins, and the other outstretched with the crop like some flying cowgirl ballerina. Of course, Tori would defy the odds and

win both classes in a row at a very competitive show, right? The thing about a jump off is that it's not over until the last person goes, and another junior phenom, Lucy Deslauriers, came into the ring after Tori. After watching Tori, Lucy put together an equally stunning performance complete with her own mad dash gallop to the final jump, besting Tori's time by 0.8 seconds and winning the class. Looking back, this event was the genesis of my enjoyment spectating show jumping, watching this duel between female riders who had yet to turn 18, each of them piloting horses over 4'9" jumps at impossible angles.[51] From here on, I would feel a rush of adrenaline watching riders career around turns and over huge standards attempting to shave fractions of a second, before watching them pass through the timers and shooting a glance up to the clock to see if they had been fast enough for the win. I had no clue what they were doing—where they were taking out strides or what their technical plan was, but I knew what time they had to beat and immediately whether or not they did it, and that was enough to get me hooked.

---

[51] I didn't realize it then, but Tori vs. Lucy could shape up to be a fascinating rivalry in the years to come—if there really are any real rivalries in show jumping. Tori probably has the edge on raw talent, but Lucy comes from show jumping progeny, is more focused on the jumper discipline and will likely have better access to horses.

CHAPTER ELEVEN

Kentucky
The Shadow of Racing

You can't spell Kentucky without horses. You can, but you know what I mean. It was inevitable that my horse show boyfriend journey would take me on my first trip to Kentucky, a state that rivals my current home, Florida, for weirdness. Everyone is concerned with horses of the racing variety while the hunter/jumpers exist as a curious offshoot to the racing crowd. They likely wonder where the foxes and betting are to make it interesting. Our destination was Lexington, Kentucky, home of the Kentucky Horse Park. It's a sprawling venue featuring large indoor and outdoor show stadiums, as well as smaller arenas and an expansive museum. It is also home to a number of equine organizations, including USEF and USHJA, the sanctioning bodies of hunter/jumper competition in the US. While they have a large steeplechase course, the vast majority of the competition is of the jumping variety here. The first show we attended was the nondescript "Kentucky Spring" show held concurrently with Old Salem in April. We also returned for another nondescript "Kentucky Summer" show in July, as well as Pony Finals and the North American Junior and Young Riders' Championships (people just call it Young Riders). These specialty events merit their own chapter later. Kentucky also hosts some prestigious things like the Rolex Three Day Eventing Championship (jumping over big logs in the field) and Hunter Derby Finals (jumping over smaller logs in the arena), which we did not attend. Having spent the better part of four weeks in Kentucky and with little unique about the "Kentucky Spring" or "Kentucky Summer" shows, the bulk of this chapter will be my attempt to explain this mystical land of horses and bourbon.

Kentucky is super confusing. An attempt to categorize it geographically goes nowhere. It was once a part of the West and is east of the Mississippi but culturally it is a long way from the East Coast. It is geographically north of "the South," but certainly has similar people and sensibilities. I think most Midwesterners would blanch at including Kentucky in their region, more so than they were already generally blanching that day. I initially compared Kentucky to Florida due to this geographical uniqueness and propensity for slightly off-kilter politicians and news-making people. I believe the only thing preventing a "Kentucky Man" meme or Twitter account is the lack of a public arrest record.

My first Kentucky acquaintance on this trip was our Airbnb host, Ken. Ken was an affable fellow with a nifty arrangement that allowed him a home near his office in Lexington and another home with his family in another nearby city where he used to work.[52] The Airbnb where we stayed was Ken's crash

---

[52] I was pretty impressed with downtown Lexington, but my basis for comparison of cities near horse shows we went to included Columbus, NC, Fishkill, NY, and Middleburg, VA.

pad, complete with an older exercise bike, vinyl records in a box on the floor and posters from bluegrass shows. At one point, Ken explained that he worked for a company that made metal chassis for automobiles, but I lost focus when I saw a Papa John's promotion on his fridge for the University of Kentucky—an archival to Papa's own alma mater and beneficiary, Louisville. Surely there must be some incongruity in the Big Blue Nation buying the pizzas that built the Cards house, I wondered, as Ken told me more about supply chains. Ken was probably our best Airbnb host on the trip because half the time he wasn't there.

Being from the South and moving to Los Angeles, I learned to value the amount of green in abundance around me whenever I returned home. However, as you might imagine, Kentucky presents a new spectrum and intensity for which I was unprepared. As we rode down the numerous backroads named pikes, I was struck by the verdant landscape and the fearless and irresponsible driving habits of everyone else on the road. Natives were content to whip around these narrow lanes at speeds far exceeding the posted limit, belying their knowledge of the area and lack of need to stop and wave at every horse sticking its head out at the fence bordering the road. We had plenty of time to do this, because the sun sets at an abnormally late hour. This is due to eastern Kentucky and Lexington being located on the very far reaches of the Eastern time zone. This made for 9:30pm dusks in the summer that were both awesome and disconcerting. We also experienced insane weather, from hellacious storms to extreme hot and cold fluctuations.[53]

---

[53] Kentucky's meteorological schizophrenia is probably a result of a deal it made with the Devil to get the recipe for bourbon.

In search of native food, I should have ceremoniously gone to a "Kentucky Fried Chicken," but it is now referred to as KFC and I pre-empted what I am sure would have been disappointment and stuck with Chick-Fil-A. Sorry, Colonel. Other than the main grocery stores bearing the pharmacy-suggesting "Kroger" name, only one new brand caught my eye—the ubiquitous cans and bottles with a bright yellow background and red on white text that screamed "ALE8." It almost looks like "Alex" when dashing by in a grocery store. I finally asked a bemused Ken about it, and he explained that it is a Kentucky-based soft drink called "Ale-8-1." I had confused the small mark after the 8 for a period of some sort instead of the minuscule number 1 that it was. I soon learned that it was essentially a caffeinated Ginger Ale, and that its name was a pun for "A Late One." I tried one and found it to be tasty, but nowhere near as delicious as my NC-native Cheerwine.

Since I didn't get to go on a bourbon distillery tour (Woodford Reserve was only 15 minutes away), I guess it's time to talk about horses in Kentucky. Kentucky has a curious relationship with jumping and other non-racing disciplines. Unlike racing, Kentucky does not seem to be the show jumping capital of the world or even the US. There are some large jumping farms and breeding operations based in and around Lexington and the Kentucky Horse Park is a gargantuan establishment, but it still feels like a very secondary sport. I took in the racing scene at WinStar Farm on my first trip and at Claiborne Farm on my second. WinStar is a fancy facility with training and breeding on 2,300 acres. I only got to see the breeding facility with the stallions, some of them very decorated winners whose names I recognized. The enormous breeding rooms where the magic happened weren't even that super creepy. Claiborne was more historical—it's where Secretariat was a sire and is currently buried. The facilities were a bit more bare bones and the breeding rooms creepier, but it was pretty neat to see the enormous paddock used by Secretariat.

I entered the hunter/jumper world with the usual general population knowledge of horse racing, and I now have a much more conflicted view of racing. I understand and appreciate the thrill of watching Secretariat dominate his competition in unprecedented fashion and was moderately excited by American Pharaoh's run, but after taking in the complexity of the jumping competition it feels more like the checkers to jumping's chess. A case could be made that racing is less a sport and more like a genetic engineering competition predicated on legal gambling. This is akin to saying NASCAR is as simple as hitting the accelerator, but with thoroughbreds the strategy seems to boil down to "do I go fast now or now." There is something exhilarating about watching all the competitors going at once and immediately seeing who wins in a short period of time. It feels like breeding is the main competition behind the sport. This, combined with the fact that a principal reason for the sport was for betting and that the horses are only used for a small period of their lives for the competition for which they are bred, makes the entire process a little less palatable. In jumping, you can watch riders and horses develop over time and conquer ever-changing courses with huge stakes against riders from other countries. In racing, you watch a perennially changing crop of eugenic masterpieces guided by interchangeable lilliputians go around in a circle in barely the time it takes you to finish half a mint julep. But racing wins the public's adoration because of its history, appeal of the simple contest and everyone's secret love of legalized gambling, drinking and big hats.

The Kentucky Horse Park houses show jumping facilities and The International Museum of the Horse, mostly dedicated to the history of the horse and the sport of racing. There are rooms full of racing trophies and one small dish engraved with the names of the Maclay equitation winners. The museum also hosts hour-long breed show demonstrations, where riders come out on all sorts of exotic breeds and the garb of their native lands. You get to see golden Ahkal-Tekes and Tennessee Walking Horses. I don't think they had any Oldenbergs that could jump 1.60m, though. Anyone that is remotely a horse person would thoroughly enjoy a pilgrimage to the museum. Just a few sidewalks away are the show rings, but very few tourists manage to wander over to see the activity. There are four main outdoor show rings with names like "Stonelea" and "Walnut" that evoke Augusta National. At places of similar size, the rings simply have numbers. There are three larger venues, one a large outdoor arena named for its sponsor—Rolex, one a smaller indoor annex arena that seems best suited for rodeos, and Alltech Arena, a large indoor stadium on the other side of the park where shows in the fall are held. Three of the smaller rings are together, and Walnut and Rolex are together about a football field's length away. Not having a golf cart in Kentucky feels like going into a High A/O jumper class with a Quarter Horse—hopeless and scary. There are no sidewalks on the roads, so you are constantly in danger of being run over as you traipse up and down the hilly landscape in what is either blistering heat or the occasional torrential downpour. It took only a short time before I began shamelessly extending my thumb to passersby when going from one ring to another. Only in rare instances did we get a ride, but it was heavenly when it happened. The spectator woes continued with the dearth of seating. Some of the rings had adjacent picnic tables and Walnut had a few bleachers, but it was not what I would call a straightforward spectating experience. The main arena, the cavernous Rolex stadium (permanent seating capacity 7,338), was rarely above 5% capacity even for the major Grand Prix events or Young Riders. Its green folding seats created something of an oven in the afternoons that led many to seek refuge in the shaded nosebleed seats. It generally only fills up for the Rolex 3-Day, the big eventing championship held in the Spring or Hunter Derby Finals held in the fall.

The big "controversy" at the Horse Park while we were there was the transition being made from white to black fences for their thirty miles of fencing. The change was a cost-saving measure, estimated to save around $50,000 a year, which could be spent on horse care rather than the more expensive and frequent painting needed for white fences. They also planned to leave the fences around the show rings white, with only the expansive paddocks surrounding the park turning black. Most barns in the area had already made the switch to black, but approaching the rolling hills of the horse park and its miles of white fences distinguished it from the rest in an iconic way. Everyone seemed to be understanding of the change but no one was particularly looking forward to it. In some ways, it illustrated the difficulties a place like the Kentucky Horse Park has in relation to other showing facilities. It is owned by the state of Kentucky but administered outside of the state park system, so any sort of improvements or changes, especially those that require money, face a considerable amount of bureaucracy. The result is a facility that in some ways shows its age compared to newer, more heavily funded ones. One example is that there is a scarcity of bathrooms in and around the show rings at the park. Those that you do find are either port-a-potties or stadium quality. Even the VIP tent was modest, with less-than-fantastic views of the Rolex Stadium and the in-ring action. There aren't many places to eat on-site and the grounds are spread out. It was difficult to understand how these problems existed just a few years after Kentucky spent significant financial capital to host the 2010 World Equestrian Games. A substantial amount probably went towards building the indoor Alltech Arena, which I only experienced small amounts of during the spring and summer shows. On the flip side, I was impressed with the areas of the Kentucky Horse Park that serve as a museum and convention area. They offer a large, equine-centric destination for people in the state most associated with horses. It feels like there is an invisible barrier between this section of the park and the section used as a horse show facility. The Kentucky Horse Park has a variety of events unlike any other, from the ones I attended (Pony Finals, Young Riders, Breyerfest) to ones I didn't (Rolex 3-Day, Derby Finals, National Horse Show). However, I was expecting show jumping to be more a part of the fabric of horse-centric Kentucky than it was. Horse racing completely overshadows show jumping, which is why it feels like Lexington could never really contend with Wellington as the mecca of show jumping. This is fine with me, as long as my next time in Kentucky I have a better place to sit and finally visit Woodford Reserve's distillery.

CHAPTER TWELVE

Upperville

Time Traveling in Virginia

After Kentucky, we spent a week in Tryon for their first FEI sanctioned competition at the new facility. Since we spent so much more time there in the summer and fall, I will skip ahead and come back to it later. The week after Tryon Spring, we finished our whirlwind 4-weeks-at-4-different-shows tour at Upperville, outside Middleburg, Virginia.

The Upperville Colt and Horse Show bills itself as the oldest horse show in the United States and takes place the first week of June. We attended the 162nd iteration of it. I had little idea what to expect as we ambled through the Virginia countryside. We entered Middleburg first, the day before the show began. It's a tiny horse-centric community a little over an hour west of Washington D.C. Like most of these places, it serves as a retreat from the big city for the elite. Middleburg addresses are so coveted that the post office has three times as many boxes (2000) as residents (751). The Kennedys had a large farm built here when JFK was president, and the town has worked hard to maintain its quaint character down to the small foxes on the street signs. Middleburg is also the home of the Chronicle of the Horse, the premiere weekly publication for horse lovers. Their website has all the latest horse news and extremely popular forums where all things horse-related are discussed. I mostly love the fact that it has a fancy sounding name, perfectly encapsulating the spirit of the sport.

The biggest recent story was the opening of the Salamander Resort north of town, a 168-room five-star resort on 340 acres. Behind it is Shelia Johnson, one of the founders of BET and an avid horsewoman. After settling in Middleburg in the '90s with her children, she decided she wanted to go into the hospitality business and bought a large parcel of land next to her barn. She then set about convincing the town council that it was not the type of unwanted development they guard against. It took a number of meetings, negotiations, and protests, but they finally came to terms, just in time for the recession to hit in 2009 and the project to be put on hold. It was finally completed and opened in late 2013.

Salamander arranged for us to do a trail ride and yoga at the barn for my girlfriend's blog. We went to check it out the day before, but there was a security guard at the entrance advising us that the entire resort had been rented out by a private party for the next 24 hours.[54] We returned the next day and took it all in. I don't often go to large five star resorts so I don't have much of a basis for comparison, but it was breathtaking. The landscape was beautiful, the barn immaculate and the equestrian touches tasteful and well thought out. I can't exactly speak to the effect that it has had on the people that

---

[54] This gives you an idea of the insane wealth of the horse show world, someone rented out a 168 room resort where rates start at $450 a night.

live in the town, but to me it certainly felt like a boon to an otherwise sleepy community. It makes it more of a destination without making the small town feel overrun while respecting its equestrian history. It's difficult to say if this is due to Shelia Johnson's vision or the town's ability to conform it to theirs, but they clearly made it work for both sides in a way that I think is beneficial to all.

The Upperville show is located about 10 minutes west of Middleburg. There is a small town bearing the name of Upperville west of it, but I did not confirm its existence. We knew we were in for a different kind of horse show when our first attempt to find it on Google Maps incorrectly put us in someone's backyard off the main road. The showgrounds are actually directly on and bisected by highway 50, the main road linking Middleburg and Upperville. Somewhat unbelievably, there are two jumper rings on one side of the road and two hunter rings on the other. During the show, police escorts stand by, ready to slow traffic if people need to walk across, sometimes while leading their horses. Veterans of the show no doubt find this to be one of its many charming aspects and would argue that some thoroughfares at WEF are more dangerous to cross. This would likely not do much to put my mind at ease if I were constantly guiding my horse back and forth over a busy highway during a show.

The showgrounds consist of two rings on each side of the highway surrounded by fields with few permanent structures. On the jumper side, one of the grass rings had recently been replaced with footing to much fanfare, but it was otherwise a fairly nondescript area with one smaller ring and a larger ring surrounded by seating for the bigger events. The hunter side was more unique, with enormous oak trees in the middle of the main hunter ring and some vintage permanent wooden seating on one side. This picturesque scene was somewhat dulled by the other side of the ring serving as the VIP parking lot, with cars directly up against the ringside fence. While it wasn't quite Old Salem's derby field (it used footing except for directly around the trees), the new footing still made for a realistic fox hunting scene for all of the specialty classes.

One thing Upperville certainly didn't lack was turn-out options. The entire area is surrounded by huge, lush green fields with the backdrop of rolling blue hills. Ironically the schooling ring on the jumper side seemed to have the best view of them. It was common to see someone with their horse out grazing during the show. Quite frequently they would just be chomping on grass in the parking lot of the showgrounds. Speaking of which—parking cost $5 a day or $50 for the whole show. This was the only show on our trip that charged for parking on a day other than when the Grand Prix was held.

Two other things that I noticed at Upperville were the great number of vendors and signs. I generally like a strong and varied vendor presence at a horse show. Old Salem had lots of different equestrian brands tastefully lined around the main pedestrian areas, while Kentucky had a smaller "Vendor Row" behind the Stonelea ring. Upperville's policy seemed to be that if there was any space within the showgrounds not being used, then they were going to find someone willing to pay to peddle their wares there. While there were a few traditional equestrian vendors, it felt a bit more like a flea market. I saw: a couple selling bags of fried mini donuts; a guy named Angus selling his "NC Ribs" from his truck; countless jewelry, hat and apparel shops; a medieval themed food establishment;

and a guy selling his fox hunting branded bloody mary mix. On the day of the Grand Prix, even more vendors set up on the other side of the ring, carting out miniature versions of their antique stores and everything else. It was somewhat overwhelming in quantity but not entirely in quality. In a similar vein, I noticed that the show organizers emulated the exuberance of a local politician in their placement of signs around the area. For the most part these signs told people NO to something, and often came in duplicate on both sides of paths. NO golf carts beyond this point. NO horses beyond this point. NO lungeing. NO touching the new grass. NO insulting the tradition of fox hunting. I managed to get a fantastic picture of a man sitting on one of the stone walls on the grounds directly in front of a sign that, in fact, told him NO to this activity.

Unfortunately, the first few days of the show experienced downpours and cold weather, making for extremely muddy paths and pools of water in the show rings. At one point, a pony hunter class resembled a moat so much that they actually had the conformation evaluation on the gravel road outside of the ring next to all the vendors. It made for some good pictures. Due to the small community nature of the show, the competition week had more amateurs, including older riders, than other shows I attended. While there are quite a few big name riders from the area, it was not the competitive scene that Old Salem was. One of the brightest stars at the show was Dr. Betsee Parker, a well-known hunter owner and a resident of Middleburg. She's like the Jerry Jones of the hunter world, except she stays out of the spotlight for the most part, providing ponies and horses to the top hunter riders of all ages. One of her beneficiaries at the show was

Tori Colvin, who was totally dominant, albeit against less competition than at a show like WEF or Old Salem. She won the $25k Jumper Welcome Stake, the USHJA Hunter Derby and two equitation classes. She even managed to get a perfect 100 score in a Large Hunter round that was sufficiently newsworthy to warrant a Chronicle of the Horse story.

The highlights of Upperville are the specialty classes, many of which I did not see elsewhere. Most shows have a lead line, where small children are lead around on horses of varying sizes and "judged," then all given blue first place ribbons. It is generally an afterthought before a bigger class. Upperville not only has the traditional lead line but a family lead line, where the entire family is dressed up and judged together. One family had the small son and father with lime green bowties and the mother with a matching lime green dress. People go all out for the family lead line, and spectators line the fence of the main hunter ring to catch a glimpse of everyone going by. They have so many competitors that multiple lead line classes for different age groups are needed. I have no idea how they find all the lead line horses suitable for this activity. At most shows they do a pretend "judging" before announcing that it's too close to call so everyone receives a blue ribbon. At Upperville they do actual judging, with the same colored ribbons that the show jumpers receive going to the top 8 finishers. Everyone else gets a participation ribbon which is truly the real prize of the event. It is the coolest ribbon I have ever seen, better than any fancy Grand Prix one, because it is rainbow colored. I'm not talking about a dull mishmash of the ROYGBIV colors or some hokey lucky charms nonsense, I'm talking about a psychedelic spectrum of the bright, almost neon version of the colors of the rainbow. You can see it in the collage on the cover of this book. I have no idea why only the bottom finishers get the ultimate prize, but I would throw my kid's lead line performance like the 1919 White Sox to get one of those.

Everyone likes seeing the pageantry of the children's lead line and the adorable miniature tack adorning the pint-sized riders, but it is just the opening event to the afternoon of specialty classes at the show. The next one featured the family class where riders from the same family all ride side by side in unison around the ring while wearing matching jackets and apparel. Then, things get even more old school with the side saddle class, where riders (mostly ladies) ride around on a horse sitting on the saddle with both legs on one side. I have no clue how this is done without falling off, especially when they all go over a moderately sized jump. It was very Disney-princess-like. Then came the fox hunters with red jackets and velvet caps, straight out of the 1900s. There were no foxes or even hounds, but they sounded a whistle and charged after make-believe foxes to the delight of the crowd. There were also a number of other events featuring specific breeds or ages of horses, where they are judged solely on conformation. One popular event was the Cleveland Bay breed class, which originated from the Cleveland district in Yorkshire, not Ohio, and is the oldest established breed in England. It was a big deal because there are so few of them left in the world, but to me it was a bunch of bay horses standing in a ring.[55] Upperville also had classes featuring foals, which were amusing because one would whinny or make a high pitched

---

[55] My apologies if I just offended the three Cleveland Bay enthusiasts reading this or the Royal Family.

squeal and suddenly cause the others to remember that they too were capable of making that noise.

Saturday night featured the big hunter derby. It was held in the main jumper ring, likely because the large VIP tent was set up there. I became immediately fixated on a jump constructed entirely out of hay bales on their sides. The highlight of the evening was an interlude in which competition was halted so everyone could rush to the nearest screen and watch American Pharaoh complete the Triple Crown.[56] The main Grand Prix Sunday brought out the whole town. A huge crowd came early for the festivities, which included a vintage car show. Watching the locals converge en masse with coolers in tow, it reminded me less of a show jumping event and more of the Carolina Cup, an annual steeplechase/college party experience held in South Carolina. One of the most amazing parts of the Grand Prix wasn't the competition itself but the fact that the organizers of the event had somehow managed to make about 90% of the seating around the enormous ring VIP-only. There were bleachers behind some of the VIP seats on one side, but if you weren't paying to watch you likely would not be getting an up-close view.

When I was first introduced to Upperville, I was still developing my idea of what constituted a horse show. It was the 5th showgrounds I had visited, and after a full year looking back it was still markedly different than the rest. It has a feel of what horse shows were like fifty years ago, lacking the modern amenities and not shedding the unique local traditions that so many others have eliminated. In some

---

[56] Of course the first Triple Crown of my lifetime happened during this very horsey year in my life.

ways it felt more like a Renaissance Faire horse show, with all the random vendors (including Ren Faire food) and a competition laden with period garb. I saw more velvet hats and red coats here than all other shows I visited. While Upperville was charming, as a spectator, I came to appreciate the ways horse shows have evolved to be more entertaining and accessible. I am not itching to go back to watch the Cleveland Bay conformation class while I stand in the mud without a seat. But, then again, I never did like Renaissance Faires or breed classes that much.

filled with local competition and the same week-to-week event schedules, Young Riders would be different. A breath of fresh air, even. No hunters or equitation. No subjective scoring. The best of the best, coming from across the country (and Canada and Mexico, I would later learn). The week in Kentucky started entertainingly enough. I went to get a carryout pizza from Dominos and noticed an SUV with a horse park parking pass on the front. As I was coming out, I poked my head in to see if they were competing, only to be greeted by the one, the only, junior phenom and Texan Lucas Porter, picking up dinner with members from the Mexican team. I can't be sure if Lucas was being hospitable or trying to poison the competition with bread and cheese, though. Lucas and his brother Wilton improbably won the junior and young rider championships respectively last year. This year, Lucas was one of a few junior-eligible riders competing in the young rider division and Wilton was sitting it out. It does not seem to be the type of event a rider tries to win more than once.

The event's formal beginning was a welcome party Tuesday night at Spy Coast Farm, a luxurious show jumping barn and breeding facility adjacent to the horse park. The tradition is for teams and riders to decorate their golf carts in wild and crazy ways, then have a "parade" from the park to the farm. Some people took this perhaps as seriously as the main competition itself, transforming their miniature jalopies into minions from Despicable Me, giant Dunkin' Donuts coffees, or cramming as many Canadian flags onto them as possible. While I took no scientific measurements, I sense the non-jumpers were decidedly more into this pageantry, a common theme of the show. I had no clue about this parade and no golf cart of my own, so I arrived to the farm at the incorrect entrance and late, greeted by a confusingly large lot of strange looking golf carts next to a packed barn. I'm still not sure how I got over the disappointment of missing the parade and was able to go on with the rest of my week.

The welcome party was not a timid affair. They had a large inflatable slide, a mechanical bull, a DJ, tents, free food, and a staple of every barn party—horses sticking their heads out of stalls wondering what in God's name is going on. There was a glut of riders in the main barn area, which I realized later was a precursor to the DJ introducing the Zones for each event. Teams at Young Riders are made up by Zones, being the arbitrary geographic region from which riders hail.[57] There were regrettably no riders from Zones 11 or 12 attending (Hawaii or Alaska). I can't even confirm they have A-circuit horse shows there. While California (Zone 10) and Texas (Zone 7) had a normal-sized contingent of riders, it was mostly East Coasters. I can't say for sure if this is due to the location being in Kentucky, the smaller number of jumpers from the west or the qualifications for the event. What resulted were scenes like a group of eight Zone 4 (Southeast) riders coming out their Zone 4 banner, soon followed shortly after by the lone representative from Zone 6, walking out to the large crowd's awkward applause. Each Zone also wore their "color" for the week adorning their matching jackets and helmet decorations. Red was popular, being used by Zones 5, 7, and 10. I believe Zone 2 opted for an understated pink; Zone 1 a pleasant green. Zone 4 was a garish shade of orange with their matching sun shirts, conjuring images of Holland. One Zone 2 rider told her Zone 4 barn mate that "Orange was

---

[57] I would at this point give you basic zone descriptions, but you can google "equestrian zone map" yourself—it's not super important.

definitely not her color" and that "she looked like a pumpkin." No love lost amongst competitors at this brutal event.

In addition to the riders' colorfulness, it was a shock to see them without helmets. After the rest of the non-hunter/jumper teams paraded out, it started pouring rain and everyone made a bee-line to the food tents. Dinner was an age appropriate selection of hot dogs, hamburgers, chicken tenders and mac n' cheese. During the rain, the DJ continued playing the music and some brave eventers (I assumed) went out and line danced, while everyone else rushed to capture the event for social media. At one point, a show jumper joined the fray and battled them in as much of a dance off as one can have at Spy Coast Farm. By the time the rain subsided, very few familiar faces remained—most of the jumpers had bolted. I was left to spectate the Mexican team engaging in various water fights and then meander over to the paddock of foals.

The competition began bright and early the next morning. There are two main divisions of competition at the event: the junior division (ages 18 and under, minimum of 14) and the young rider division (ages 21 and under). The only difference between them is the young rider division's jumps are slightly higher. Part of the appeal of Young Riders is that it is one of the few events for riders under 21 that uses Nations Cup style scoring. There are three days of competition consisting of five rounds, all done on one horse from which the rider must accrue a certain number of points to qualify for the event. There are no jump offs, and the scoring is based on the number of faults accumulated over the rounds.

Day 1 (Wednesday) features one round and a complicated scoring system. I would spend 3 sentences telling you about it, but it would be exceedingly boring.[58] The conventional wisdom is that you want to play it safe on the first day, such that normally aggressive riders saunter around the ring taking no chances whatsoever so they don't knock themselves out of competition.

Day 2 (Thursday) features two rounds of team competition that also serve as additional qualifying rounds for the individual competition. Riders are divided into the aforementioned teams by Zone, with 4 riders to a team. The rounds are scored based on how many faults a rider has, so the main goal is to go clear under the time allowed and not amass any jumping or time faults that will add to your score. The best score you can get is 0, and the top 3 scores for each team's round will count towards the team's final score. This means one rider can royally screw up their round and the team can still be okay because their score will be dropped. The team with the lowest score after two rounds wins. Each individual rider's scores will also be added to their computed score from Day 1 and carried over to the final day of individual competition.

Day 3 (Friday) has a short farewell competition that combines riders in the junior and young rider divisions that didn't qualify for the final day of individual competition and has a lower jump height overall (1.30m). Participation in this is optional for riders that didn't qualify and is scored with a normal jump off.

---

[58] The reason they make it so complicated is they want every rider to have a point total with some decimal places to avoid ties in the final competition, since all the other numbers will be based on jumping or time faults, which are only in multiples of 4 or 1. I can feel your excitement about the intricacies of the scoring system.

Day 4 (Saturday) is the final day of individual competition, where riders have two more rounds that are scored the same way as the team competition day, and only faults count towards their score. The rider with the lowest score from all five of their rounds wins the individual championship. On the final day the riders compete in reverse order of placing, with the rider in first going last. There is no benefit to going faster than any other rider during the final four rounds as long as you stay under the time allowed.

Going into the first day, I expected to see a high level of jumping by a group of the country's top riders on their best horses. Instead I saw something of a pillow fight. There were very few sharp turns or risky decisions as most experienced riders opted to take the safe route. The less experienced, happy-to-be-there riders generally had less than stellar first round performances that would undoubtedly knock them out of the individual competition. It was somewhat gut-wrenching to watch riders who regularly post champion ribbons have trouble in one meaningful round. The first day's action was held in the Walnut ring at the Kentucky Horse Park, so if you didn't have a golf cart to park along the side of the ring, there was not much in the way of seating. The rest of the competition (other than the farewell event) would trade the asymmetric confines of the Walnut for the cavernous Rolex stadium.

With the first day under wraps and the scoring system not making sense to me, I tried to prepare for the team competition by scanning the rosters. The way the team competition works is if you don't have three riders from your zone to make up the minimum amount for a team, they put two zones together. This led to some team "Zone 7/9" and

"Zone 3/5" combinations that made the team combinations a little less meaningful. The camaraderie among some teams was strong, though—all the Zone 7 junior team members were from Texas and at the event for their first time. They clearly were having lots of fun together. Riders on such a team do their best to try not to disappoint their fellow teammates with a bad score and ruin their chances of winning, even though they may barely know each other. There were also lots of riders we hadn't seen from the west coast and Canada/Mexico to watch, including the daughters of the two tech moguls Steve Jobs and Bill Gates. I, being a Mac guy since birth, had my rooting interest secured. My girlfriend, notoriously bad at recognizing faces, asked me early on if I thought Gates would be there. I took the opportunity later in the week to point up to a man in the stadium seating on a laptop and whisper excitedly to her, "Oh my God, that's Bill Gates!!" and letting her believe it for at least five minutes. We would actually meet him at another show, though.

Another first for me at Young Riders was attending an event being widely covered by other equestrian media outlets. I was not used to having a media center or publications alongside the ring taking redundant pictures. In some ways it was my own version of a competition, taking the best picture and putting it up the quickest. I would later be further ingratiated into the usual cadre of media at WEF, where an occasional betting pool took place for the Grand Prix classes.[59] It was an interesting group of people, being all female and with a sufficient passion for horses enough that they chose a profession covering them. I think a lot of horse media people

---

[59] At some of the major events sponsored by Rolex, they do a media betting pool and award the winner with a nice bottle of champagne.

are also eventing riders because it's cheaper, or because they are slightly crazier. I was able to learn how others worked and what they thought was interesting and worth covering. For example, multiple publications posted pictures of riders' horses after they had fallen off—one going over a jump without its rider, one running around the ring under the scoreboard proclaiming its then-ironic name: Catch Me T. Both entertaining moments, but not something my girlfriend or I would choose to share on her outlet, especially with captions detailing the falls and naming the riders as these did. I felt vindicated when we were later asked by an upset team chef d'equipe if we were with the publication that posted one of the pictures, as one of his riders had been distraught by it.

As I slogged through the team day trying to keep up with the teams and standings, I slowly realized that the anticipated big-time competition among the junior riders had been neutered by the don't-screw-up mentality of the Nations Cup format scoring. The main strategy for victory is to play it safe and just make it around the course, as scores are counted only by rails down and time faults. There is no incentive to go faster than anyone else as long as you stay under the time allowed. You can only lose in competition by knocking down a rail—winning is simply based on not losing. While this does make for tense, pressure filled rounds, I would have rather seen the top riders go all out to beat each other. It was disappointing when I learned that the biggest events in the sport, the Olympics and WEG, are scored this way. The team day ended with some generic zones taking the top three places, medals and places on podiums, followed by an awkward press conference and even more awkward forced mid-air jumping team victory picture. I appreciated the irony of making the riders jump after the horses jumped. This would be like making the jockeys at the derby do a 40-yard dash after winning.

Competition the next day was more of the same, except slightly shorter since the fields had been pared down somewhat. About half of the competitors had little chance of winning because of the mathematical hole they were in. For the second day, the abundant stadium seating at the Rolex stadium was mostly empty save for relatives, and quite a few opted for the shaded nosebleed seats. It was not exactly the desired atmosphere for a top-level sporting competition. As I watched the individual competition play out, I realized that the championship event I was seeking for the sport I was getting into didn't really exist at a junior level. Sure, riders wanted to win this, but the primary purpose seemed to be to give future professionals a taste of Nations Cup competition and scoring rather than crown an actual junior champion. It just wasn't as important as I was expecting, a feeling that was validated the next year when the competition moved to Colorado and few top East Coast riders attended. But at least the year I attended it was a unique melange of equestrian disciplines coming together from across North America. Having said that, I am not in any hurry to sit through another three days of watching risk-averse riding.

CHAPTER FOURTEEN

Breyerfest

I'll Stop Collecting When I'm Dead

We interrupt this journey through the hunter/jumper A-Circuit to bring you a brief and unexpected interlude into my travels. While attending Young Riders at the Kentucky Horse Park in late July, there was another, very different event occurring simultaneously on the grounds. It was Breyerfest, a 3-day annual convention for lovers of Breyer model horses, that is, small plastic toy horses. Before I offend anyone with such a reductionist description, I should note these are much closer to handcrafted pieces of art than crappy toys from Walmart. While they are mass-produced, there is still a level of craftsmanship in their design. A traditional Breyer costs anywhere from $25 to $50, not exactly inexpensive but still a cheaper hobby than owning a real horse. Most horse lovers grow up collecting or at least owning a few of these toys, but Breyerfest represents the culture at its peak. It attracts nearly 10,000 people. A three-day ticket for children 12 and under goes for $67.50, while for everyone over 12 tickets are $97.50. The cost of admission does not include accommodations, parking, or the many, many items available for purchase there. I attended the 26th annual Breyerfest in 2015 (it is as old as I am). Every year there is a theme for Breyerfest around which the events are organized. This year's theme was "Vive La France," and the Celebration Horse was a French Ardennes Stallion.[60] As with most of my horse travels, I had prepared myself for an adequate level of horse-person strangeness, but it was no match for my introduction to Breyerfest.

Since Young Riders started earlier in the week, we had ample prior warnings that Breyerfest would be huge and crazy. We heard that people would line up at 5:00am on Friday morning to ensure they were first to get the yearly Breyerfest celebration horse given to all attendees. I decided we didn't need to arrive at that early to get the full effect, so we showed up shortly before the gates opened at 9:00am. The first indication that this would be a different experience was in the parking lot, where many cars had decorations notifying all that they were headed to Breyerfest 2015. We saw lots of "Breyerfest or Bust!" signs and even more creative window decals of horses, with license plates from all over. I soon found myself in the midst of a throng of Breyer-obsessed people browsing the many vendors or waiting in line for the privilege to purchase special run limited edition Breyers available in small quantities only at this event. Where the culture of the A-circuit hunter/jumper scene is like fine wine, with nuanced notes of formality and elitism, Breyerfest's culture is a bucket of water to the face of pure, unadulterated devotion, fanaticism and commercialism.

---

[60] This Breyer was included in the ticket price and is on the cover of the book. It was pretty cool looking even if stallions scare the bejesus out of me.

I first noticed snaking lines for purchasing limited edition Breyers, for which the organizers had mercifully constructed tarps and fans for relief from the hot sun. I eventually found myself inside the covered arena, where 47 vendors were set up ready to cater to the masses. There were smaller, independent Breyer stores that specialized in older models and would buy or trade your collectables. Some of these were densely organized with boxes stacking ten to twenty feet high, others just had out-of-box Breyers haphazardly standing side by side on tables in large clusters. One vendor called "B&B Hobby Kids" had a crudely printed sheet on their sign with a shiny brown blob on it. Upon further inspection, it touted their willingness to trade or pay cash for Colton or Logan, with a picture of a bull. Apparently this was an extremely rare Breyer model Hereford bull released in 2012—only 40 were made. No word on if they ever got their Colton or Logan.[61] This seems like a good time to mention that Breyer is not just about the 1:9 scale model horses. They make smaller 1:32 scale horses called Stablemates and other various sized ones, as well as every sort of horse accessory you could imagine, including entire barns and facilities. They also make other animals that are barn life, like the aforementioned Hereford bulls. My immersion into the hunter/jumper world has made it seem very outsized, but being in Breyer-land reminded me that it is only a very small part of the horse world. Their products represent all disciplines and breeds. Some

---

[61] Out of morbid curiosity, I found that these sold for $150 at release and I saw one on eBay from a year ago for $520. They have all sorts of limited edition models for people who join collectors' clubs and attend and volunteer at Breyerfest. The prices of these can skyrocket—a one of a kind glossy model of the 2008 Celebration Horse, Alborozo, sold at a charity auction for $13,500.

enterprising young collectors have found that Breyer does not offer the specific accessory they desire, so they, usually with the help of their fathers, create them themselves. This results in some of the Breyerfest vendors being father-daughter combinations selling homemade stackable stables or customizable model horse jumps. I don't think I saw people having any more fun than these families running their business together around the daughters' passion and fathers' craftsmanship.

Breyerfest is not only about getting everyone together to buy a bunch of model horse stuff. It's also a "Celebration of the Horse." There are small shows featuring all sorts of breeds and disciplines going on throughout the weekend. In the brief period I was there, I witnessed vaulting (acrobatics on horseback), horses pulling carts in unison and horses with flamenco-style dancers. There were a number of different horses out for attendees to interact with, including some of the ones who had been immortalized into model form. There is also significant encouragement of creativity at the event, most prevalent in the model horse show. Attendees are invited to make a diorama featuring Breyer horses around the theme of Breyerfest. The dioramas I saw on display were not the cobbled together catastrophes you might turn in for a school assignment. They were painstakingly detailed scenes that could have taken weeks to craft. Some of these mystifying scenes included Parisian cafes with horses enjoying champagne, a Monument à la République Breyer, and an impressionist French painter Breyer.[62] Attendees continued

---

[62] I later learned that the prize for these model shows is a special prize model Breyer, which is probably the rarest of these limited edition ones available. Needless to say the competitors were a little more motivated than your average High Jr/AO Classic.

the theme in their apparel, wearing everything from elaborate French costumes to custom t-shirts emblazoned with their social media accounts dedicated to Breyer collecting. Breyer knew how to cater to their audience too, selling a slew of different clothing from the yearly themed options to the generic shirts proclaiming, "I'll Stop Collecting When I'm Dead."

There were a cornucopia of Breyer and non-Breyer related activities, from workshops on collecting and model horse showing to Splash Dogs, a competition in which dogs jump as far as they can off a ramp into a large pool of water. Easily my favorite activity at Breyerfest was one of the most popular—Stablemate painting. They had a large tent where you could get your very own blank, white Stablemate and paint it yourself, for free. This tent was packed, and everyone was painting a Stablemate—kids, parents, grandparents, random 20-something bloggers only there because of a jumper show. Everyone was huddled around tables intensely focused on their own 1:32 scale masterpieces. I overheard one father saying, "of course I'm going to paint one, I paid enough to be here!" My first Stablemate was, to put it mildly, not the pinnacle of artistic achievement. I didn't have much idea what I was doing and we were a little pressed for time. After marveling at my girlfriend's work, I knew I had to return. On Sunday we wandered back over to the tent, as crowded as ever, and I proceeded to slave over another Stablemate, splashing it with all hues of the rainbow in various spiraling swirls and designs. As I profusely sweated among a crowd of other artists perfecting their model equine masterpieces, I began to understand the Breyerfest spirit that had perplexed me only days earlier.

My only experience growing up with any similar obsession was with Pokémon. I played the video game and collected the cards for a brief period, going to one or two events where one battled with the cards. This gave me a small understanding of the collection aspect, but I never went to a large Pokémon fan gathering, nor was I able to meet a Pokémon in real life (maybe some day).[63] At Breyerfest, watching the attendees interact with the real, live horses which served as models for these collections, you would think they were meeting a Pikachu in the flesh. There were copious amounts of tears, gasps and just general wide-eyed disbelief. It makes sense that someone who spends a majority of their time collecting plastic horse figures probably doesn't get an opportunity to be around horses frequently. When they do, it is something of a religious experience, especially if said horse is in any way famous. This is where I was struck by the insane juxtaposition of the two horse events taking place a mere football field's length from each other. At Young Riders, you have people who not only have been riding for a good portion of their childhood, but can afford a horse that can jump at a professional level for a sustained four-day period. It is the 1% of the 1% of the horse world. On the other side, you have people who love horses, but may not be able to afford them or even be around them on a regular basis, so they collect small model versions of them with a vigor that brings them to this yearly gathering.

I do not dispute riders' love of horses—you certainly would have to at least enjoy interacting with equines to make it this far in the sport. Very likely a long time ago riders regarded the

---

[63] I wrote this before Pokémon Go came out. Me playing it probably delayed the release of my book a month.

mere presence of a horse with a similar wonderment. For most riders such wonderment morphed into an ultra-competitive sport and upscale lifestyle where they barely crack a smile after a clear round or win. Despite my nascent love affair with the sport of show jumping, it is easy to be disillusioned by its ridiculous economic barriers to entry and the love of glamour trumping the love of horse for some. The Breyerfest interlude was a welcome respite from this, but it also made me realize show jumping's potential as a sport. If I can get into it as a spectator without having any previous predilection for horses, then surely this vast army of Breyer fans would appreciate the finer points of show jumping, wouldn't they? In some ways, the easiest path to affordability for show jumping is maximizing its fan base and participation. The more there is demand for an affordable path to the sport, the better chance it has of creating wider appreciation of the sport. I would love to see all the Breyer fanatics have my introduction to the hunter/jumper world and become rabid McLain, Beezie or Tori fans. But for now, as the top juniors maneuvered around the Rolex Stadium aboard their half-million dollar horses, Breyer fans congregated en masse in celebration of their $35 models next door in two worlds that couldn't be more far apart.

CHAPTER FIFTEEN

Pony Finals
What am I Doing Here?

Without question, when telling equestrians of our show schedule, the one that elicited the most emotional reaction was Pony Finals. At one point, my girlfriend and I were doing a recurring post on her blog called Horse Show Faces, an offshoot of the popular blog Faces of New York and we recorded this exchange between two riders about Pony Finals during the spring leading up to it:

Girl 1: I actually did Pony Finals here (at Kentucky) and my pony tried to run out the in-gate. I was like, "No! I'm only 11! Be nice to me!" Yeah, there's a lot of crying.

Girl 2: Yeah, there's a lot of bows, glitter.

Girl 1: And a lot of moms braiding hair.

Girl 2: And this is when you see all the dads. All the dads flock out. They have no idea what's happening. They just wander around. You can tell they've never been here before. They're so touristy. It's really cute.

Girl 1: There's a lot of colorful socks too. I feel like that's when you're really into colored socks.

Girl 2: There's a lot of colors. A lot of energy.

Girl 1: There's a lot of energy. Negative and positive.

In some ways, I wish this was the end of the chapter on Pony Finals, and I could say something about how accurately this describes the spirit of the show and I decided to sit out what would be the fifth horse show in six weeks for me. But alas, I made the treacherous journey to Pony Finals and now must share the burden. As I mentioned in the prologue, attending Pony Finals was my "maybe I should be justifying this by writing a book or something" moment. So you have Pony Finals to blame, not only for your scarring experience there as a small child, but also for this book.

Pony Finals is a six-day championship event for all pony competition, held at the Kentucky Horse Park in Lexington. Some 400 riders and 600 ponies compete in hunter, jumper and equitation classes. The hunter classes are the large draw here, taking up most of the competition time and entries. Otherwise, there is a highly regarded equitation class on Sunday morning and the pony jumpers have a more modest competition. Riders and ponies must meet qualification requirements to gain an invitation to the event, but they are not terribly difficult. For the hunters, the pony must be a champion or reserve champion in a class to qualify for that class at Pony Finals. The size of the show where they achieve this does not matter. Even the person riding the pony is irrelevant, as once the pony qualifies they can be leased (for a tidy sum) to another rider wanting to go to Pony Finals but unable to qualify with his or her own pony. So it's a kind of exclusive championship event in which anyone can compete and hundreds of people do so.

Now is a good time to remind the non-horseperson enjoying this book that ponies are not, in fact, baby horses, but are fully grown, smaller sized horses. It is amusingly common for the horse to be older than its rider. Most of the pony riders range in age from 8 to 14, but the official cutoff is 18. As with most junior competitions, the riders are 99% female. Much like with the big horses, the Pony Hunter competition is divided into Small, Medium and Large by size, and consists of three classes in which all ponies in their division compete—model, under saddle, and over fences. Each division requires an excruciatingly long half day to complete in order to accommodate the large number of entries. There are winners in each class and an overall grand champion for the entire division, based on scores from the cumulative results. Each class is very different and has its own quirks and strategy.

The model division is the beauty pageant. Horses are judged on conformation, soundness, how they move and how mean they are. I made up one of those. Because this is Pony Finals, an immense amount of work goes into making these horses look fantastic. Grooms carry around these small wooden carriers full of mysterious bottles and cans to prepare the ponies before going into the ring. I found myself learning about all sorts of horse grooming products, such as Show Sheen, a hair de-tangler with a distinctive scent that makes the horse's mane and tail look as if they've just exited the salon. Then there's the hoof dressing, a concoction that I saw most frequently in an old-timey yellow can that is painted onto the horse's hooves to make them shine, something apparently positive to a judge.[64] The combination of these two smells with the heavy doses of citronella applied to the horse's coat results in a chemical cloud rivaling the perfume counter at Belk's. Observing the army of people dolling up these ponies, I noticed the other battle of model showing: getting the pony to stand still and behave. The top horses, the veterans of Pony Finals, needed little cajoling to go into the ring and stand still, but some unfortunate pre-teenage girls had to practically drag their equine "friends" into the ring and beg them to stand still for the judge and their big moment. One can almost convince themselves this competition is an invaluable educational moment for a young girl, having to briefly care for another sentient being as part of a high level of competition, justifying its astronomical cost. Then you realize you could just get them a dog and learn the same lessons.

After the model division comes the only slightly more exciting under saddle, where groups of riders ride around the ring, taking commands from judges primarily to change their speeds. This is part dance performance and part demolition derby. While the presence of other competitors in the ring during the model presents little issue, under saddle requires you to deftly navigate for space and position among your other tiny, bow-laden sisterhood, all while making sure your horse obeys your commands to trot, canter and do the hokey pokey. One of the tricks of the under saddle at all levels is to circle the ring faster but slow down at the portion of it closer to the judges to get more close-up time in front of them and make an impression. This results in occasional traffic jam cut

---

[64] Rudimentary research tells me this hoof dressing is 91% mineral oil. I have no knowledge whether a groom has ever had to resort to using hoof dressing personally for help staying regular.

offs. Having said all this, to the uninformed, this will appear to be merely a bunch of horses being ridden in a circle around the ring. Much like the model, I would have about as much of a chance predicting who won as I would jumping the 1.40m class next door in Rolex Stadium.

The final portion of the competition is the over fences, or the actual jumping of a course. It's a testament to the pageantry and frivolity of the hunter competition that only one third of it involves jumping a horse. And for pony hunters, it's less jumping and more slight hopping, since the jumps are barely knee high to an adult. This presents some interesting dilemmas for photographing the event, as there is much less opportunity to photograph any jump in mid-air. They also have comically intricate jumps for their size, including an iconic large faux wrought-iron gate. This, along with the large "US PONY FINALS" sign above the usual scoreboard are must-have photo backdrops for all attendees. After the round, there's a worthy photo moment for riders when their score is posted on the scoreboard for their proof of showing. One rider, upon exiting the ring from her round to hugs and kisses brushed them off with frantic motions for the camera shouting "SCOREBOARD, SCOREBOARD!!" By the time the over fences has happened, two other events have been scored, so the riders come back in reverse order of score. This results in the first 60-70 riders having somewhat inconsequential rounds, as even a high score will not put them in the top 10 or so overall. This, combined with the fact that the entire event contained minimal amounts of actual jumping, contributed to the absurd nature of the show.

The action in the hunter ring during the four days is repetitive, never ending, robotic and confusing. It is more suitable viewing as a torture device than a spectator sport. When people reminisce about Pony Finals, as did the two ladies at the beginning of this chapter, they are more likely to discuss the before and after pageantry around it. So much effort is expended to attend, qualify and compete in classes in excess of a hundred riders with little hope of success that the young girls, their families and trainers experience much angst. One sees all sorts of emotions and pep talks upon entering the ring—from the standard "do your best" to singing the lyrics to Taylor Swift's "Shake It Off" in unison. Upon the rider's finish and exit from the ring, there is a corresponding emotional release of excitement or disappointment, depending on how the round went. Combining this emotional volatility with the fact that the in gate and schooling ring is more crowded than at any other show, due to the number of competitors, makes for a high energy spectacle. Now, add all the colors. It is very common for young girl riders to have their hair come down in pigtails out of their helmets with bright, unique bows at the end of them. I saw bows with lobsters on them, SpongeBob bows, Florida gator bows and bows with hues of the color spectrum I could have only previously experienced while under the influence of psychotropic drugs (something that would have enhanced the experience of Pony Finals).

One of the common threads of everyone's Pony Finals story is the crazy parent (mother). No Pony Finals experience is complete without having a rider's mother acting or saying something crazy. They even had a "Pony Mom Land" hospitality area away from the show which offered complimentary massages, comfortable seating and, yes, a happy hour. The mere presence of the Pony Finals fathers is cause for amusement, as they are a rarity at horse shows and had the misfortune to be dragged to this particular event. Through their confused evaluation of the action, you can see them counting the seconds until they can escape to a bourbon distillery down the road for the much needed sampling tour to forget about how much this is all costing. Also present were the usual groups of bored horse show brothers. This left my presence at the show in a sort of strange limbo. A few other women in their early twenties were present covering the show. I am certain I was the only adult male between the ages of 20 and 35 there. I would say my presence was met with some sidelong glances, but nothing is strange at Pony Finals.

Another memorable experience occurred when I checked in the media tent upon arrival. It doubled as the merchandising area and was being swarmed like a grocery store before a big storm. Most of the Pony Finals gear sold out on the first day, in spite of the ridiculous prices. Making sure everyone knows you went to Pony Finals through apparel and pictures is way more exciting than actually being at Pony Finals.[65] If you didn't spend enough at the merchandise tent, they also had a pony auction. The pony auction is a little strange, since most of the good ponies are sold based on their performance in the ring and tried beforehand for fit. The ones that have to be sold at auction are arguably a bit less nice. I knew the auction would be riveting when we were told at the beginning to "be sure that you are bidding on the pony that you want. This is important."

---

[65] I would imagine it's sort of like the Masters in golf in this regard. And there goes my golf-loving audience. Hey, we both know you go for the gear and cheap food, not to stand around in the Georgia heat wishing Tiger was good again.

The auction took place in the cavernous Alltech Arena at the Kentucky Horse Park. This is where the jumper and equitation events took place. There is only one major pony equitation class—Pony Medal.[66] Pony Medal finals takes place on Sunday mornings, and very rarely do unknown ponies or riders do well at it. I lasted about ten minutes watching it because of the monotony of the rounds, so that's pretty much all I can say on the matter. Pony jumpers is a totally different competition. Occasionally there are pony jumper classes at shows, but they rarely are full events and for some reason aren't encouraged in the US. The Pony Finals class was relatively small and frequented by riders I was not familiar with. Pony jumpers has a much bigger following in Europe, where it is the main class for children and hunters are done sparingly, if at all. Probably the best thing about pony jumpers was hearing the hunter competitors talk about it. The general consensus was similar to that of a NASCAR race. People were excited to go watch due to the high probability of riders falling off and/or crashing. Such hazards are common with pony jumpers, as it seems to be the more affordable alternative to hunters. As a result, you have young girls attempting to navigate small, often inexpensive ponies over larger sized jumps while going hilariously fast relative to their size. While regular jumper classes seem like an orchestrated balance of speed and grace, pony jumpers bear resemblance to a pinball machine. We watched most of the event and it was terrifying. Every successful jump felt like a minor miracle, and the faults and dismounts were as abundant as our hunter friends had predicted. There was a stark difference in the level

---

[66] Apparently the Pony Maclay and USEF Pony Talent Search classes have yet to materialize. I sense an opportunity.

of competition between it and the hunter division. It makes little sense to me that the jumper competition is overlooked at the pony level before becoming more standard at the junior and professional and amateur levels.

More than the other shows I attended, competing at Pony Finals was a big deal to all the riders there. This was the event hundreds of young people had worked towards, and the emotion and energy was palpable. I saw more hugs, tears, special outfits and smiles than every other show combined. I personally wish everyone competing was able to do so in a less subjective scoring format, that offered better chances of success to more riders. However, I am probably the only one clamoring for this change. Most riders are content to qualify, attend the show and get their picture jumping in front of the "US PONY FINALS" sign. I could now tell you that for me Pony Finals was about as torturous as it gets—I didn't understand what was happening the entire time. Classes were never-ending and non-VIP spectator conditions were dismal. But for this show, it wasn't about my experience, it was about the pony riders.

CHAPTER SIXTEEN

A Mini Interlude
Peeps and Her Posse

About halfway through my horse show journey, Peeps came into my life. Peeps is a miniature dwarf chestnut mare with pink hair. A miniature horse is what it sounds like—a very small but fully-grown horse. They are smaller than most ponies (usually no taller than 34-38 inches) and have more horse-like dimensions and characteristics. A dwarf miniature horse is simply one with a dwarfism gene that causes it to be even smaller. While I am sure there are breed shows for them, the vast majority are pets, mascots or lawn ornaments with no competitive activity. In the hunter/jumper world, miniature horses can serve as companions in the field and stall for larger horses, improving their mood or condition. Like my girlfriend, Peeps was Instagram-famous and we had been following her escapades since WEF. We wanted to do a story on Peeps for my girlfriend's blog, but had not caught up with her until we were back in Kentucky for Pony Finals, where we met her on vendor row one day. She was impossibly small and sassy, and we scheduled a time to come by and meet the rest of her crew at their barn off site.

Peeps's "dads" are Josh Dolan and Alex Granato, two professional hunter/jumper riders a little older than me with a show barn based out of Wellington. Josh and Alex were in Kentucky for a show in the spring of 2014, driving on a back road when they passed a barn with a dwarf miniature horse in the field that appeared to be in bad shape. The entrance was padlocked, so they went down a neighbor's road and saw more than 60 minis behind the barn. They hopped the fence and went into the barn, where they saw a starved mini lying dead in the middle of the aisle and many others in dire conditions. They immediately called Animal Control and the police. Over the next few days they couldn't find the property owner or do anything about the situation. They returned and noticed the situation had worsened with many of the minis, so in a last-ditch effort they pinned a note on the gate with a number saying they were interested in purchasing some. That night, they got a call back from the owner saying he was willing to sell, so they went back the next day. They learned that he used to breed them but had let the situation deteriorate. Josh and Alex bought 19 minis that day and transported them back to their barn, where they set about finding room in their full show barn to temporarily house them and nurse them back to health. They started calling all their show jumping friends to find homes for the minis in better shape. To begin, they rescued and found homes for 35 minis—all because they saw one dwarf out front: Peeps. They ended up keeping Peeps and a few other special ones at their show barn.

Peeps was just a yearling when she arrived at their barn, Mad Season, LLC, and had not developed many of the problems that plague miniature dwarf horses when neglected. Their conformation can become greatly affected, causing their front feet to turn inwards and make it difficult to walk. The first few weeks in her new home went smoothly for Peeps, but she soon developed Rhodococcus equi, a serious and deadly condition affecting young horses. In order to fight it, she was confined to a dark stall and kept on antibiotics for months. The fun-loving personality she had developed at her new home was soon replaced by a constant depression and sadness from her illness and confinement. She had shown little signs of improvement after four months, and it was time for the Mad Season crew to return to Florida for the winter. Everyone was concerned that Peeps wouldn't be able to make the long trip in her weakened condition. Josh and Alex had been caring for Peeps for almost 5 months at this point and they were determined to bring Peeps with them. They set up a special box stall in the trailer all to herself and successfully transported her to Wellington. Shortly after arrival, the antibiotics started to work and her condition improved. She was cured and became sassier than ever, so the crew dyed her hair pink and started an Instagram account for her. After attending a few of the Saturday Night Lights events at WEF, Peeps became a celebrity. With their experience rescuing Peeps and the other minis, the Mad Season crew realized they had a passion for helping these small horses in need, and they began looking for more of them to rescue, rehab and re-home.

When I arrived at their barn in Kentucky, they had 8 minis wandering around in the field out front, like it was a scene in an equestrian Sound of Music. It was unbelievable. There were five regular miniature horses and three dwarf ones, including Peeps. The other two dwarf ones had serious movement problems. One black one, Tiny, was a four-year-old mare with little mangled legs that turned in all sorts of directions except the right ones. Standing was a struggle for her, let alone moving from place to place. Another dwarf, Swirl, was a pinto gelding that was even smaller than Peeps and Tiny and couldn't stand up at the time. He was equal parts excruciatingly adorable and heartbreaking. Josh and Alex were working to help Swirl and Tiny get the proper shoes and care so that they could move better. We took a hilarious group picture of them with their entire barn, all eight minis and Alex's retired Grand Prix horse. Up to this point, my comfort level around horses had become a little more relaxed, but I was still reticent to interact with them. Being kicked or bitten or having pain inflicted on me by a creature 15 times my size was always in the back of my mind. This fear evaporated when I was around a miniature version of them. I could approach and play with them with ease, and it set me on a course of being able to interact with the equines I had come to spend so much time with.

We kept in touch with Josh and Alex and happened to cross paths with them again during the fall shows in Tryon. Since we had met them, we had been brainstorming ways to help them with the minis. While in Tryon, we became friends and they graciously offered my girlfriend a chance to ride a few of their horses at the show. While she had ridden once or twice before this, this was the first time she was able to consistently ride a couple of times a week, and it was easily one of the best parts of the year for her. I can only imagine how difficult it was to go to all the different shows but only watch something you love doing for the better part of the year. I decided the best way to return their generosity would be to help them with a goal they had mentioned to me in Kentucky—the creation of a non-profit dedicated to rescuing and finding new homes for miniature horses in need. I set about creating a website and filing the paperwork for what would become The Peeps Foundation, named after the pink-haired mini that started it all.

A couple of months later, the foundation was up and running and the requests to adopt minis poured in. I greatly enjoyed the process of meeting new minis as they came in, befriending them (usually with the help of mints), and seeing them off to their new homes and excited owners. Some of the minis were more difficult to approach and handle because of their trauma, so it was always rewarding when they became a little less hesitant. I initially struggled with some of the basics, like putting on a halter and leading them around. Only the mischievous minis took advantage of my naiveté and made things difficult for me. Peeps in particular had a fun habit of running away from me in the paddock when I was going to put her halter on to return her to her stall, only to come to the gate on her own if I dared leave. I did learn a few lessons in my first few ventures adopting out minis. One prospective adopter was coming by to look at the two minis available for adoption. Peeps and the rest of the permanent crew were back near the big horse stalls. Josh and Alex were doing some work on their fancy mini paddocks, so Peeps and the other minis were in a makeshift paddock area behind one of the rows of stalls at the time. I was out front with the rescues up for adoption when the woman with whom I had been communicating drove up in a golf cart with another female friend. I met them both, but I didn't catch her friend's name because she was speaking with a European-type accent. They met the two rescues and asked if they could meet Peeps. Not remembering that they were not in their normal paddocks and stalls, I brought them back to see them. They found them playing around in the mud in their makeshift area, a situation which, in retrospect, made it look like we were the ones who the minis needed to be rescued from. Josh and Alex, who happened to be there, immediately started talking to them about the minis and apologizing for the scene as they were working on their permanent home. They chatted with the prospective mini owners for quite a while, giving far more attention to them than most visitors. Eventually the guests left without finalizing an adoption for the day, and Alex pulled me aside and told me to make sure to let them know when we were expecting people so they could clean up a little more. I had actually let them know earlier that day and it hadn't been an issue with the others I invited to visit the minis. The problem was that the woman's friend with the strange accent was, unbeknownst to me, actually Athena Onassis, the granddaughter of Aristotle Onassis. Athena is one of the most famous and wealthy professional equestrians, even hosting her own annual horse show that bears her name on the beach in Saint-Tropez, and she had just been to our barn to see the minis when it was not at its tidiest. The woman I had been communicating with was her groom. That taught me to do even more research before meeting someone. One of the minis from that day, Gummy, did get adopted a week or so later, and a barn owner and her 5-year-old son came by to pick him up. I was the only one at the barn, so I went to retrieve him from the stall where he and his other

CHAPTER SEVENTEEN

New Albany

The Perfect Horse Show Day

"The party tonight is being held at the Car Barn" is very high on the list of statements I was not expecting to hear during my year of horse shows. Yet, there I was, wandering into an actual barn containing around twenty vintage Ferraris. While there is a linear progression of events that led me to this point, the existential question of how exactly I got here hung over me as I tried not to spill champagne on these multi-million dollar red pieces of art.

The collector of these Ferraris was Leslie Wexner, the wealthiest person in Ohio at a net worth of $7 billion, who made a good bit of his money through various retail stores such as Victoria's Secret, Bath & Body Works and other various mall staples. His wife, Abigail, is an equestrian and show jumping owner of many of Beezie Madden's top horses. In 1998, she started a one-day charity horse show held on their sprawling estate in New Albany, Ohio, a suburb of Columbus. The show has evolved to a large one-day family fair event centered around the horse show that draws all the top riders on the North American circuit. It is as close to a perfect horse show day as possible. It has everything: top-level competition, a beautiful setting with a great course and field, and a huge community draw around live music, rides and all sorts of activities. Oh, and the best part? It's all for charity. The proceeds from the event go to The Center for Family Safety and Healing, a non-profit organization that was started by Mrs. Wexner and dedicated to stopping family violence. In the event's 20 years of existence, it has raised over $30 million dollars—all from a one-day horse show. About 18,000 people attend each year and another 350 volunteer to work at the event. The experience of the show and its scope was even more awe-inspiring than the Ferrari-laden surroundings of the party the night before.

We decided to go to the New Albany Classic because one of the organizers of the event invited my girlfriend to come cover the Classic after seeing her blog. Of course I would say so, but it says a lot about New Albany's forward-thinking leadership to recognize the impact of my girlfriend's blog and how it could benefit their show to make sure that she attended and covered it. Now, I could be talking about how great New Albany is because they paid us to be there, but many other people who had to buy a reasonably-priced ticket to attend will corroborate my proclamations of its high rank among well-run shows.

We arrived on Saturday, the day before the event, and before the party we had one other piece of business to attend to. My girlfriend had been slated to be at a meet and greet at a local tack store. They were actually advertising her presence as a way to get people to come, which both of us found surreal. On the way over, she fretted about her horrid signature in case autographs were requested. Upon arrival, it turned out to be less pressure than we had envisioned, as two younger local riders were also there to meet and take pictures with fans. But my girlfriend did end up meeting, signing autographs and taking pictures with people who came out to see her. The day would only get more surreal as we headed to the much-anticipated Car Barn party. It's difficult to accurately paint a picture of the venue, but just imagine a vintage Ferrari museum inside of an extremely nice barn. You walk in, see a room with a handful of Ferraris, then turn the corner to find yet another one. It's one of the few barns that houses something that make show jumping horses look inexpensive by comparison. As I walked around examining each Ferrari without being able to tell much difference between them, I expected someone to come up and politely ask me to leave because I was not supposed to be there.

The event was primarily for the riders and VIP sponsors, maybe 200 people in total, and we were all at assigned seats for dinner. Our table was less occupied than most. I made conversation with a gentleman from JP Morgan and resisted the urge to ask him the secrets to making gobs of money. We were then joined by none other than Richard Jeffery, the course designer for the event. Every major horse show has at least one course designer, sometimes many more for the separate disciplines or just the classes in the Grand Prix ring. These folks are a mercurial group, tasked with creating a challenging course for riders that have seen everything while also ensuring that it is easy to set up and to go from one class to another for a bigger show. I had met a few designers before, but had not been able to talk with them about the craft and about show jumping. I didn't know it at the time, but Richard

Jeffery is probably one of the most accomplished course designers in the world. He's won the USEF Course Designer of the Year award 7 times, does big events like the World Equestrian Games and the Rolex Three-Day Event and has designed every New Albany course since its inception. In person, he was an affable Englishman willing to entertain all of my prying and silly questions about the sport. Most memorably, when I was asking him about reconciling complaints over a course's difficulty, he responded with the advice: "don't bring a 2* star horse to a 5* star event."

We finished our delicious meal and headed home, but not before receiving a basket of fresh produce from the farm on the estate on our way out. We were catching a flight to NYC Monday morning and suddenly had a basket of fresh fruit and vegetables in the trunk of our rental car that couldn't possibly go to waste. Luckily a friend from high school and his wife visited us Sunday night after the event and took it, saving us from having to pull an all-nighter to eat entire squashes.

We arrived the next morning about an hour before the doors opened at 10am. There would be four hours until the Grand Prix and I was already regretting all the show's aspects I would not be able to capture. There was an unbelievable amount of activity. The crown jewel was an exhibit of dinosaurs from the Jurassic Park movie, complete with a large 30-foot-tall animatronic T-Rex skeleton outside the tent greeting visitors. Their regular attractions included ten different huge rides you might see at a fair, a zip-line, petting zoo, rock-climbing wall, car show, arts and crafts areas, a pumpkin patch, a synthetic ice skating rink and hay-rides. A smaller performance stage featured a talent show, short plays and a ballet. There were people dressed up as characters walking around the show, including Darth Vader and Chewbacca. If all this mayhem and activity wasn't enough, there was a concert going on most of the time. The event brings in a lot of up and coming teen bands. In the past they've had the Jonas Brothers, Demi Lovato and Ariana Grande. This year they brought in RaeLynn, Before You Exit, and Timeflies. I had heard of none of them before, and after, I was a fan of all of them—they were fantastic and had the crowd going wild. Once lunchtime came, they had eight food trucks to serve the crowd. If anything, I am leaving out some of the amazing things they had to do and see, and it was a perfect fall day. Because we were there covering the event, we had access to the VIP tent where delicious, healthy food was served. Much of the food was grown right on site at the estate. They even had an area for kids with activities and their own food, as well. With all this going on, it was difficult at times to remember that there was actually a horse show later in the day and all these people were here to see it.

By the time the show started, I was exhausted in the best possible way and ready to start taking pictures of the beautiful course and packed stands in the background. The show takes place on a luscious grass field that is used once a year for this event. The riders take a winding path from the schooling ring through a small wooded area to the ring. Inside the ring, they had the most interesting and creative jumps, including one with a bag of golf clubs and flag and an upturned bucket of balls and a beach-themed one with sand, chair, umbrella and a tiki torch. It is an FEI 2* star invitational Grand Prix with prize money for the riders, and it draws lots of the top riders from the US and abroad. Beezie Madden was the crowd favorite because she always rides a horse owned by Abigail

Wexner in the event. She had a chance to win in the jump off, but couldn't catch the fast time set by Conor Swail and had to settle for 2nd.

If you can't tell from my breathless description, I thought New Albany was awesome, and it appeared that the thousands of people who attend yearly and the riders that regularly rank it as the top specialty show in North America are of the same opinion. They have built-in advantages over the WEFs of the horse show world. It is for one day with one class of showing on a field that is used once a year. They can invite whom they want to compete, and structure the show around a huge day of activities that lure people into being interested in expensive horses jumping over the same course over and over while raising a lot of money for a good cause. After attending many other horse shows, it would be interesting to see where the sport would be if it had the widespread organization and appeal that it does for one fall day in the middle of Ohio.

CHAPTER EIGHTEEN

Central Park

Bright Lights, Wild Horse Show

So, Donald Trump, the Pope, Beyonce, Bill Gates and the Queen of Dressage, Charlotte Dujardin walk into an ice skating rink covered in footing. It sounds like the premise of either a bad joke or a good psychedelic drug trip, but it was neither. It was the 2015 Central Park Horse Show.

Out of all the horse shows I attended over the course of the year, the Central Park Horse Show was by far the most eventful. It took place inside the ice skating rink (Wollman Rink) at the south end of Central Park in New York City. The show is an ambitious and complex undertaking, with mind-boggling logistics involved over the course of the week of events that leave you aching and exhausted by Sunday evening. It is a specialty one-week show in its second year put on by a partnership headed by Mark Bellissimo, who also oversees WEF and Tryon. The inaugural Grand Prix in 2014 was appropriately won by Georgina Bloomberg, the daughter of the former NYC mayor Mike Bloomberg. Georgina is an accomplished rider who has represented the US in Nations

Cup competition and in the Pan-American Games. I saw her at the introductory press conference out of riding attire on the Tuesday before the show. It was more like seeing a famous person than any other rider. While she had the requisite savvy with the media, her most salient attribute was her superior posture, which was by far the best I had ever seen in person. Forget her riding ability and horses, I would kill just to be able to keep my chin up and shoulders back like her. Georgina is probably the closest thing young equestrian girls have to a role model, or as the kids say these days, "goals." She also has an adorable young son, who after the press conference drove around in a mini Land Rover in the ring, providing me with the best pictures of the week.

The existence of the Central Park Horse Show is rooted in two main desires: to provide a unique venue for the top show jumpers to compete in; and, to expose the city to show jumping. The latter of these also is meant to draw non-equestrian sponsors to a well-off audience, and this is why the show is heavily adorned with references to Rolex, Land Rover and JetBlue.[67] There is also the goal of bringing back show jumping to New York City, as it used to host the once-prestigious National Horse Show at Madison Square Garden before it moved to Florida, then Kentucky over ten years ago. In Central Park's second year, it has supplemented its two Grand Prix jumping classes with a cornucopia of other events including amateur and under-25 jumping classes, hunters (professional, amateur, and ponies), dressage and Arabians, as well as a master class with Charlotte Dujardin. It was a whirlwind of activity from Wednesday to Sunday as these

---

[67] Still waiting on my Submariner, Range Rover and trip vouchers for this mention, guys.

things unfolded. Before I go into the gory detail of each, allow me to set the stage for the venue.

Because I had never seen the place as an ice skating rink, seeing it now covered in footing with jumps and surrounding VIP tent seating seemed perfectly normal to me. There had been a massive, round the clock effort to get the venue ready, and when I arrived on Tuesday it was finally coming together. The rink is surrounded by trees and foliage that eventually give way to the skyscrapers of midtown, so you aren't totally engulfed by the architectural scenery as you are on the beach in Miami. The riders walk their horses from the schooling ring at the Central Park baseball field, under the cordoned-off pedestrian bridges across the park and into the ring. The scale and density of the ring's setting made it difficult to get photos that adequately showed the landscape, the skyscrapers looming far above and riders negotiating the six foot jumps.

One of our early-week tasks before the show was to get pictures of a new George Morris Breyer action figure we were helping to promote. It had a number of phrases recorded by George built in, admonishing your riding ability. We used this as an excuse to see some of the city and took pictures of him on Top of the Rock, with the Statue of Liberty and with an NYPD cop. Being the horse people we now are, we also went to eat at Ralph Lauren's Polo Bar, where reservations for a very early dinner were required about two months in advance. The food was decent and the atmosphere was decadent and equestrian-themed. I am fairly certain the waiters knew I wasn't rich; they can smell it on you. Between the distance to the ring from the hotel and these activities, I severely underestimated the amount of walking involved. By Thursday, I was in Duane Reade looking for a shoe insole and blister band-aids. They conveniently had them near the counter taunting tourists like me. I still developed a terrible pain in my right foot that bothered me off and on for months. I think next time I will use a hoverboard to get around.

The show schedule was Arabians on Wednesday, the under 25 and speed jumper classes on Thursday, the amateur and Grand Prix classes on Friday, then hunters during the day on Saturday followed by dressage at night and a Pony Club competition and Charlotte's dressage master class during the day on Sunday. Starting on Wednesday we had a 10am to 11pm non-stop day at the ring covering the event. They had a nice media area overlooking the ring and provided decent food, but I had to take time out to sample some of New York's finest delicacies—including a Central Park vendor's hot dog, Momofuku Milk Bar and 99 cent pizza. Each event was ticketed with temporary bleacher seating surrounding the ring and two VIP areas above them. While the bleacher seats may have had better views than the VIP, they were not cheap. The ticket prices varied depending on the event, with some in the $30-50 range for the Arabians and hunters and up to $250 for the Grand Prix events. It was almost impossible to watch the event without a ticket outside the show, though you could stand on the far side of the park behind a barricade and watch the horses go into the ring. They also had free ticketing for the Sunday morning event featuring riding demos and the Pony Club competition. The ticket prices are definitely a sticking point for the future, but the event itself costs upwards of $3 million to put on. You can't blame them for charging to attend, especially since it is the only show they do charge for, as Wellington and Tryon Grand Prix events are always free.

If this action-packed schedule wasn't enough, the week of the show also happened to be the week that Pope Francis visited New York City. His entourage came right through Central Park and the area in general. In addition, there was a free concert taking place on Saturday in Central Park featuring Beyonce and Coldplay, among others. My parents also happened to be in town on vacation the same week. Fortunately, these events did little to affect the show, though on the day the Pope came through they had closed off the entire park and only we could gain access to the show that afternoon, so that was a little eerie. My parents happened to be walking a few blocks away when the Pope rode by in his black Fiat, inadvertently getting closer to him than many people who had waited all day to see him. Il Papa also managed to ride behind the schooling ring in the park, and a number of photographers got on a forklift and took a picture of Charlotte Dujardin in the ring with him going by in the background. It would have been great if the pope had decided to come sit in the VIP for the show, but I would imagine he had a strict schedule.

Speaking of VIP, while all horse shows have VIP areas, this one had actual VIP famous people attending because it was in New York. One of our tasks was to attempt to clandestinely photograph them while they were watching to get some proof they were there for the tabloids. I am not a paparazzi, and this task was unbelievably difficult and took away from the shooting that needed to be done ringside during the event. The first night, Donald Trump was present. Donald is no stranger to horse shows, having hosted one at the Mar-A-Lago earlier in the year. It did not happen again in 2016, for obvious reasons, so I was unable to document it. His organization also runs the activities at the Wollman Rink where the Central Park Horse Show took place. At the time of this show in September, Trump's presidential campaign was picking up steam, but that night he was likely just another spectator amused that he had gotten so far in the race.[68] We didn't dare try to get any sort of picture of him. This displeased the PR agency, so the next night we had to get at least one famous-person picture to mollify them. Luckily my girlfriend knew Jen Gates, who was riding in the under 25 and amateur classes and whose family, including her father Bill, was in attendance. Jen was extremely nice and accommodating (she also had just won the amateur class), and we went up to the VIP to take their photo during the break. As I approached them, they were all standing and talking except Bill, who was doing a little dance to the music they were playing. I would probably dance often if I were him. They were very gracious as we quickly snapped their picture.[69] The final night, during the dressage competition, Ann and Mitt Romney were in attendance. Ann is a dressage enthusiast and their ownership of an Olympic dressage horse (Rafalca!) was much-discussed during Mitt's presidential run. I can't speak to agreeing with his politics, but I could certainly empathize with Mitt's status as a Horse Show Husband. I can imagine him discussing the latest dressage-related expenses with Ann in the same tone that he discusses the need to cut taxes.

---

[68] I had a note here that read "make amusing joke about how he can now retire and run horse shows exclusively after he loses the election." Oops.

[69] I had to resist the urge to ask him if they actually had skipped from Windows 8 to 10 because of the coding errors it would cause for old programs having a Windows 9 with a Windows 95 and 98. Also I wanted to know if he too enjoyed a competitive jump-off as much as I did.

The show's first evening featured an Arabian horse showcase. I don't think I had ever been around an Arabian horse before, let alone seen a competition involving them. Arabians are a totally different type of horse than the breeds used in dressage and general show jumping competition, and it is apparent as you get closer to them. The main difference is that Arabians are hot-blooded, while show horses are warm-blooded, and working or draft horses are cold-blooded. These names are meant to confuse weak-minded and unknowledgeable people like me, who naturally assumed at first that they had to do with the actual temperature of the blood coursing through the horse's veins. They instead refer to the horse's general temperament and body type. For example, hot-blooded horses are excitable and sensitive, light-weighted and quick. The two main hot-blood breeds are the Arabians and the Thoroughbreds, being the horses that you see on the racetrack and occasionally in the show ring. Cold-blooded horses are large, strong and resistant, and are predominantly used in labor or pulling carts and include breeds like Clydesdales or Fresians. Warm-bloods are the mix of the two: medium sized, not too excitable or calm and perfect for the show ring. I can see where you could infer from the name what their personality is, but perhaps they should opt for less literal names for these horse types so as not to indicate any sort of actual biological meaning. Plus, it's just kind of silly to me to refer to a scientific grouping of a horse by some euphemism for upsetting quickly. We might as well call hot-blooded horses "short fuse horses."

Arabians are a big deal, with quite a bit of money being put into showing the breed's top horses. But, between the type of the horse and competition it couldn't be more different from show jumping. First, Arabians are terrifying. They look and move like wild horses, and even after attending numerous horse shows you could not cajole me to within shouting distance of one. They are a little smaller and have tails that shoot up in the back like a fountain. The competition I saw consisted of handlers in coats and ties leading them out by a lead rope and running them around the ring in an extremely frenetic fashion. They stop occasionally and do something like tussle their mane or fix some part of their appearance that may have become disheveled, then run them around again. At some point they use a long whip to direct them into doing some form of dancing or eye movement, ostensibly to show some level of training. I wouldn't say it was necessarily doing tricks like you would with a dog, but it was a similar demonstration. I had little idea of what was going on and even less of an idea as to how these men ran around in suits while guiding these terrifying creatures that could easily outrun them by 30mph. The Arabians tended to develop these shiny films on and around their mouths, which was either saliva buildup or some form of vaseline being applied to them. Either way it was weird. Another class featured competitors actually riding the Arabians while wearing hilarious suit, tie and hat get-ups. It was more confusing than dressage, but with more action. The evening concluded with a costume contest, where the riders wore traditional Arabian garb. Again, I had no idea what was going on and still don't, other than it was very odd and I now know these horses don't actually have literally warmer blood than other horses. We staggered back to the hotel around 11:30pm, starving and with about 3,000 pictures of Arabians to edit. This was day one.

I was in more familiar territory the second day of the show as show jumping was featured. There were two classes in the evening—an under 25 class and a speed warm up for the Grand Prix the next night. Nicole Bellissimo, Mark's daughter, won the U25 event in dramatic fashion as the final rider to go in the jump off; and Conor Swail, fresh off his win at New Albany the week before, won the speed class.

Friday was the first day that featured a matinee afternoon competition, and it was a dressage event. Up to this point I tried to avoid dressage competitions, or as some like to call it, horse dancing. The horses went out and danced, the riders got super excited when their routines were over, there was a big rectangle, it was dressage. If there wasn't music, it would be almost impossible for the average person to sit through. One amusing moment came when interviewing Charlotte Dujardin, hailed as the "Queen of Dressage" from Britain who had recently won all the big dressage events—World Cups, Olympics among other horse dancing championships. She had never been to New York City until now. When asked about her first visit to NYC, she said she was very excited to take in the sights like the Statue of Liberty and the Eiffel Tower. We had to do that take over. She was hilarious and very British and is so good at horse dancing that she constantly had small girls rushing up to her asking for her autograph.

Friday night was the big jumping show. It started with a 1.20m Junior/Amateur class for the people who paid large sums of money to hop around the small jumps under the skyscrapers. For the second week in a row I was treated to a class full of top riders, but the course had other plans, wreaking havoc and causing faults everywhere. It was fairly tight and probably a unique atmosphere for most of the horses. The most jarring event of the evening was witnessing McLain and Rothchild have a refusal twice on the same jump[70]. Only two out of twenty-seven riders made it to the jump off—Sharn Wordley and Daniel Bluman. They are both affable fellows from New Zealand and Colombia respectively. Sharn had the unfortunate luck of going first, an incredible disadvantage in a two person jump off. He kept it careful but recorded a slower time, so Daniel sped quickly around for the victory, removing his helmet after the last jump in jubilation as he rode in front of the stands. Sharn would later say in the press conference that when Daniel realized it was just the two of them in the jump off, he tried to bargain with him trying to get him to agree that the 1st place winner would get the prize money and 2nd place would get the Rolex watch that the winner was supposed to receive. Sharn then jokingly demanded the watch. That was only the second best moment of the evening. During the podium ceremony, Daniel was given a bottle of champagne, and during the photo session it exploded behind the top three finishers on the podium. This didn't deter him from taking a big swig and spraying it on Sharn and the third place finisher, Shane Sweetnam. After the dust settled and as they headed to the press conference, Sharn reached over and took a long swig of the champagne. Shane motioned for him to come on up to the press conference, and Sharn decided he needed another long chug of champagne before heading to meet the press, giving me one of my favorite pictures of the week.

---

[70] After this happened, I glanced over at Lisa Slade, shooting for the Chronicle next to me and we both had faces like we had just seen a car accident.

The excitement of Thursday and Friday night gave way to a day of boredom on Saturday: hunters in the afternoon and dressage at night. They tried to make the hunter classes as interesting and spectator-friendly as possible. This effort included a "freestyle" Pony Hunter class in which the pony kids got to pick their own song for their ride to similar to how the dressage freestyle works. There were some amusing and fitting choices (Welcome to New York by Taylor Swift), but my personal favorite was the one girl riding to "Worth It" by Fifth Harmony, the chorus of which is "Give it to me I'm worth it, uh-huh I'm worth it." The best thing about the hunter competition was that they had a graffiti artist create NYC-inspired art to go with the usual brush and stone jumps seen on a hunter course. The coolest thing I had seen in a hunter ring before that was Upperville's enormous hay bale jump. Saturday night meant more dressage competition, this time under the lights. I again had very little idea what was going on, but everyone seemed to be enjoying the horse dancing, including the Romneys up in the VIP.

On Sunday, they opened up the stadium for a free show featuring a jumping demonstration and a Pony Club competition. Pony Club was something I had not previously seen. It is an all-encompassing program featuring horsemanship, teamwork, service and education about horses. While they compete in a variety of ways, that morning we saw two teams do a series of relay competitions. They each had elaborate uniforms and funny names like "Camo Girls" and "No Brakes, No Problem." The events included popping balloons on horseback, handing off relay cards and getting on and off your pony at a moment's notice. They even had to drive the mini Land Rover cars at one point. It was way more fun to watch than the hunters or dressage.

The afternoon featured a dressage master class with Charlotte Dujardin. Her usual Olympic mount couldn't make the trip, so she was riding a new horse to her that was equally as famous, making her flawless presentation even more impressive. It was a very informative session that I promptly forgot most of because I wasn't exactly going to go apply it in the dressage arena next week. I do remember her saying that she liked a hot horse instead of a lazy one because she liked to guide the horse's energy instead of using a lot herself to get it moving.[71] This event was just one of the many I attended that hundreds of horse people would give their horse's left haunch to attend.

Central Park was many things, but above all it was very interesting. It had many elements uncommon to the A-circuit scene, such as Land Rover mini cars, Arabians and graffiti jumps. It was an otherworldly show, with all sorts of different horse disciplines, and it was exhausting, going on almost an entire week of non-stop specialty show action. In addition to the action in the ring, this was the only horse show where I was in the presence of two queens (Beyonce and Dujardin) a pope, the richest man in the world (Gates), and a respectable Republican presidential candidate (Mitt Romney).

---

[71] I feel the same way about my girlfriend... I think.

CHAPTER NINETEEN

Tryon
Log Cabins and Air-Conditioned Bathrooms

I glanced down at my phone as we traversed a stretch of highway between Asheville and Charlotte that was unfamiliar even to me, a North Carolina native. The cell service bars ticked away as we crept further from discernible civilization into the foothills of the Blue Ridge Mountains. We passed villages with made-up sounding names like "Forest City" and "Rutherfordton." Finally, we turned off at the newly minted exit sign for Tryon International Equestrian Center, where we found no gas station or anything except miraculously returned cell service and a large American flag in a gravel lot. Pulling up, the valley below came into view, a massive showgrounds surrounded by dense forest. It was an amazing sight with the showgrounds being half a new and pristine equestrian complex and the rest under construction. To be able to take it all in from a high vantage point felt like you were playing SimCity Horse Show Edition. At the time it was only the 3rd show after WEF we visited, so I hadn't fully experienced the quaint backyard/fairgrounds aspect of horse shows that still persists in some A-circuit shows. After returning to Tryon in the summer and fall, I realized just how much the showgrounds was dropkicking the old status quo and ushering in a new, resort-like frontier for the horse show world in which I had become immersed.

The town of Tryon, NC is about 50 minutes southeast of Asheville and a little over an hour east of Charlotte. One of the many small equestrian enclaves dotting the East Coast, its heyday was long ago when it hosted the 1956 and 1960 Olympic trials for show jumping. It still had a fox hunting community, but major show jumping competition had long since left. Enter Mark Bellissimo (of WEF ownership) and his investment group, who are in the process of building one of North America's premiere equestrian facilities. For full disclosure before raving about this brand-spanking new facility: my girlfriend is currently employed by the company that runs both Tryon and WEF. So while my opinions on them might be a bit biased, how Tryon and WEF are being developed by their owners is also a reason she chose to work for them.

The most common description of Tryon is that it resembles a horse show Disneyland. Some mean this positively, others negatively. It is far more developed and offers an all-encompassing experience some are not used to in a horse show. There will always be purists for whom horse shows are rings with small buildings in the woods and regard Tryon's enormous show grounds warily. But most riders seem to appreciate the modernity and effort put into the place. Tryon currently is a facility with 7 show rings, including one in a stadium that holds 6,000 people. It has a derby field and a cross country course, as well as a large covered ring. There are a number of restaurants on site, including an old-fashioned diner, an Italian restaurant and an upscale bar and grill. It has on-site 1, 3 and 5 bedroom cabins and permanent stalls directly next to the show rings. It looks and feels like an amusement park, and it is awesome. Even now, in its incomplete state, it would rank as one of the premiere equestrian facilities in North America. The speed at which it is being developed is unprecedented. In the middle of 2014 it was literally a forest in the middle of nowhere. While we were there, construction happened overnight, paths were paved, buildings materialized and things looked different week to week. They brought in pre-fab log cabins for all the on-site housing and vendor areas, giving it a mountain theme park feel. They even had shuffleboard next to the lodging, which my girlfriend and I made use of on numerous occasions.[72] Future plans include several resort hotels, shops, condos, farmettes (small farms on the showgrounds), an outdoor amphitheater, a mountain bike trail, and a chocolate waterfall.[73] As many winning riders observed during their press conferences when asked about Tryon: "it's going to be the place to be."

While the showgrounds are evolving, the Center is still very much out in the middle of nowhere. The showgrounds are technically in Mill Spring, NC, though the "town" of Mill Spring is really just a stoplight about 10 minutes away. Another 15 minutes will put you in the towns of Columbus, Tryon, Forest City or Landrum, SC, where you can get gas, fast food, and eat at some passable restaurants. The closest

---

[72] As I previously mentioned, I'm actually 75 years old. But shuffleboard is awesome and I love whoever is responsible for it being at Tryon.

[73] I made up one of these. Farmettes aren't a real thing.

Chick-Fil-A is a half hour away, but there are, no exaggeration, over 30 Baptist churches within a 10-mile radius. For anything more than this you have to venture almost an hour away to Asheville or Greenville. I grew up in a similarly rural area in central North Carolina, so this was not a jarring proposition for me. It was exciting to be close to the mountains and Asheville instead of a crappy lake and Winston-Salem. But for equestrians who spend much of their time in the Northeast, Florida and even overseas, Tryon might as well be the wilderness. One of the biggest issues with Tryon is lodging. They have plopped down a huge number of cabins and RV spots, but at peak capacity it doesn't begin to house all the exhibitors attending the show. From there, the only options are rentals close to the show grounds, as there are only basic 2 star hotels in the nearby towns. Between our summer and fall visits they built a very nice motel just off show grounds, but it was not gargantuan and barely put a dent in the lodging demands. There are large plots cleared for resort hotels and condos that will surely spring up faster than imaginable, though.

Tryon was one of the first shows I attended where I felt like I wasn't being tortured spectating a horse show all day. It may be the result of Mark Bellissimo spectating his daughters' shows and being dissatisfied with the experience. Every ring has elevated, shaded seating with oversized outdoor furniture (not bleachers) with great views. There are huge, air-conditioned bathroom cabins everywhere. Nothing beats walking into an igloo of a bathroom complete with marble countertops on a scorching show day.[74] There are pedestrian

---

[74] I should mention at a horse show it always feels 10 degrees hotter on a hot day and 10 degrees colder on a cold day.

walkways around all the rings, so golf carts are unnecessary and parking is easy and close by. I could go on forever listing all the small and enjoyable things about Tryon: phone charging stations, hammocks, a silo bar, a general store with local items and a fitness center. All these things seem small and semi-irrelevant until you spend a lot of your time at other shows scouring the area for a port-a-potty, trekking up a hill with no sidewalk to go from ring to ring, and eating overpriced fair food for lunch. These amenities make is easily the most boyfriend-friendly horse show I visited. They even have a ton of activities nearby to keep non-horsepeople occupied, such as boating on Lake Lure, golf, hiking and breweries in Asheville (including the new Sierra Nevada one). My personal favorite outing that my girlfriend and I did multiple times with our show friends was tubing on the Green River in Saluda. It is at least as scary, unpredictable and fun as jumping a horse, but quite a bit more wallet-friendly at $9. The downtowns of Tryon and nearby Landrum in South Carolina are also quaint and somewhat equine-themed. A favorite restaurant of ours in Landrum is The Hare and Hound, a pub-like venue with tons of equestrian decor and fantastic food.[75] One of the biggest benefits to Tryon's location is its proximity to the South Carolina border, as South Carolina has much cheaper gas and alcohol.[76]

Tryon also imported the Saturday Night Lights Grand Prix event from WEF and Wellington. At WEF it feels like a large portion of the audience is VIP and horse people, but at Tryon almost all of it is local townspeople who may or may not still

---

[75] When my girlfriend showed for the first time in 9 years, it was at Tryon and decided at 11pm the night before after many drinks at the Hare and Hound.

refer to it as a race. In the two hours leading up to the event, they have free carousel rides out front and feature a number of performers (magicians, bubble blowers, jugglers), face painting, pony rides and many other activities. Parking and admission are free, and the community comes out in droves. As they have returned, their knowledge of the sport has increased, to the point where they now cheer loudly when riders have a clear round or groan when they have a rail down. Other attractions come with the event, including a band that plays on a stage above the arena every week. Country singer Lee Greenwood has appeared several times and has been a big draw. He sings the "Prrrrroud to be an Amurrrican" song that apparently people in rural NC go crazy for. Going with the patriotic theme, on several occasions there were parachute jumpers landing in the stadium with flags during the national anthem. I certainly got my share of entertainment which the owners provided to attract people to watch horses jump.

One of my pet peeves about professional show jumping is riders who are stoic after winning a big Grand Prix. It's rare enough that they go last in a jump-off and know they've won after they finish, so I am irritated when riders just do a small wave to the crowd or even less upon clinching victory. At Tryon, the extremely active crowd seems to inject life in the riders, who are always much more excited performing in front of them than any other venue I visited. Not only do riders do fist pumps after winning jump-offs at Tryon, but many celebrate with the crowd after simply going clear. My two favorite memories of this happening are from two riders based nearby. I didn't know of Fernando Cardenas before seeing him in his first few Grand Prix events at Tryon. He is not only a professional rider representing Colombia but also a full-time equine veterinarian with his own clinic in NC. During the spring of 2016, he and his horse Quincy Car were trying to qualify for the Colombian Olympic team, so the stakes were high for him to do well at the Tryon Grand Prix events in which he was competing. When Tryon held its first 5* Grand Prix, Fernando had his own personal cheering section full of his veterinary clients holding up homemade signs. He performed a fantastic clear round and immediately started celebrating afterwards, doing a windmill motion with his arm while gesturing wildly to his cheering section. I realized later when I looked at a picture I had taken of him mid-celebration that he was so exuberant he was about to fall sideways off his horse. After this, I awaited his jump-off round with great anticipation. He did not disappoint, submitting a clear jump-off round to take the lead followed by another big celebration. After rewatching the video and looking at the pictures of him celebrating again, my new goal in life is to feel as happy about anything as Fernando does about a double clear round. I would be remiss if I didn't also mention one other passionate celebrator I encountered at Tryon, the local boy, Andy Kocher. Andy very much breaks the mold of the typical professional rider and is always a mix of excitement and terror in the ring. During a Fall 3* Grand Prix at Tryon, Andy completed a blisteringly fast double clear round that would win him the class. In addition to his normal post round celebration, he actually raised his arm in mid-air going over the final jump, as if he was on a mechanical bull. I'm not sure if it was intentional, but it was unbelievable and even more hilarious in a photo later.

Much like in Kentucky, I experienced a large cross-section of equestrian competition at Tryon. Most of it was after my girlfriend was hired by them rather than during our initial barnstorming tour, and it included the Pony Club Championships and American Eventing Championships. These two events were vastly different than a hunter/jumper show, as they used the newly constructed cross country course and were more spread out. I found it more difficult to follow the action, but the scenery was breathtaking. It had more of a steeplechase vibe to it. All I really remember from Pony Club was the walking-around outfit of choice being paddock boots and shorts and the crazy stall decorations everyone did. Much like Pony Finals, there was lots of energy. I even saw cool hunter/jumper moments like Tryon's first FEI sanctioned show and 5* Grand Prix and Brunello's Breyer model ceremony (then subsequent victory for the first hunter derby on the new derby field). The constantly evolving Tryon was the ideal horse show to see so many new and different things happening over the course of my first few years in the sport.

Tryon represents progress in a sport where so many events and shows are content to keep doing things the way they have always been, emphasizing their history rather than their future. From the moment I stepped on to the show grounds, my mind was blown. I had no idea a place that hosted horse shows for half the year could be like this. The craziest part about Tryon is it isn't even close to completion. A sign of Tryon's rising status came in November 2016, when it was awarded the 2018 World Equestrian games, only the second time it will be held in the United States. Tryon has much yet to do, but considering what they have accomplished since 2014, don't bet against them.

CHAPTER TWENTY

Shows I Didn't Go To

But Felt Like I Should Mention

Before I continue on to the last few shows, I wanted to take a brief moment to detail a few major horse shows I didn't attend. Most of these were near the end of the circuit calendar and would appear at this point chronologically in the book. I couldn't go to every show; some overlapped (summer shows), some were financially not possible (Hampton Classic) and some were too scary (Capital Challenge). The majority of the shows I didn't attend are part of the so-called indoors circuit which starts in October and takes place in covered arenas mostly in the northeast. They are notable for hosting the different kinds of equitation finals, none of which I attended in person. If I did go to one of these eq finals, the chapter would probably read something like:

"I woke up at 6am and went to a musty, cavernous arena that is probably better suited for a rodeo show. I did this so I could watch 250 teenagers walk a course from a high vantage point, which made them, dressed up in their show jackets and breeches, look like a horde of penguins milling around frantically. I then watched all of them go in a row, non-stop for days on end, doing the same boring course. I had no grasp whatsoever of the competition but at least knew that probably half of them should not have wasted their time and money attending. I mostly feel sorry for the judges and press that have to watch all the rounds with some level of attentiveness. There is no way they make fraction of the money the trainers here make. I can't wait to do it all again in 1 to 3 weeks."

That's my faux-take from indoors. If you're a family member, it is probably best to try to find an excuse not to go and just watch it on the livestream at home and not think about how much money you are spending on it. Here are those and the other shows I didn't attend that most would say are notable on the A-circuit schedule.

DEVON

When: End of May

Where: Outside Philadelphia, PA.

What: A two week show, with the first one being juniors-only with big equitation and hunter classes.

Why you would go: Historical value, unique show arena slathered in UNC blue, lemon sticks (lemons with sugar sticks in them that you post on Instagram).

Why you wouldn't go: Crowded schooling ring (singular) where you may run in to a saddlebred horse piloted by a semi-competent elderly rider not wearing protective headgear. No FEI Classes.

SPRUCE MEADOWS

When: May to September
Where: Calgary, Alberta, Canada
What: A sprawling showgrounds consistently regarded as one of the best in North America.
Why you would go: Big classes, lots of prize money, beautiful landscape, strict on-time ring schedule, cross it off your horse show bucket list.
Why you wouldn't go: Is very expensive.

HAMPTON CLASSIC

When: End of August
Where: Bridgehampton, NY (on Long Island)
What: A weeklong show that includes a number of local classes.
Why you would go: It's summer in the Hamptons! Luxurious VIP, tons of vendors, World Cup Qualifier FEI Grand Prix, you're a New Yorker that only competes at Old Salem and here every year.
Why you wouldn't go: The logistics (stabling, lodging, parking) leave something to be desired. Very hoity-toity. If you're not rich, they might find out and burn you at the stake or take you out on their yachts and make you walk the plank.

HITS

When: Year-round.
Where: Three large venues in Ocala, FL, Thermal, CA (mostly winter shows) and Saugerties, NY (summer), in addition to smaller shows in Arizona and Virginia.
What: A horse show company that manages a group of shows across the country.
Why you would go: Closer proximity than other competing shows, lighter competition, $1 Million Grand Prix events, slightly smaller show fees.
Why you wouldn't go: Lighter competition, tagged by some teenagers as "SHITS" because of less than luxurious amenities compared to the other shows (probably half-valid).

CAPITAL CHALLENGE

When: First week of October
Where: Upper Marlboro, MD (30 minutes east of DC)
What: A horse show with both indoor and outdoor rings regarded as preparation for the indoor circuit.
Why you would go: Competing in Taylor Harris or Adult Medal equitation finals, because you or your trainer have always gone.[77]
Why you wouldn't go: Held in a very sketchy area for the horse show crowd, referred to by many riders as "Capital Punishment."

---

[77] I was told to think of it "like the one relative that you don't like seeing but your family forces you to visit them once a year."

PENNSYLVANIA NATIONAL HORSE SHOW

When: Around the 2nd week in October
Where: Harrisburg, PA
What: One of the first horse shows on the indoor circuit, split into a junior and adult week.
Why you would go: Medal Finals. Scenic industrial Harrisburg in the fall.
Why you wouldn't go: Because you are not competing in Medal Finals.

WASHINGTON INTERNATIONAL HORSE SHOW

When: Last week of October
Where: Verizon Center, Washington DC
What: Known as WIHS, a large one-week horse show.
Why you would go: Large-scale production with unique events (puissance/high jump, barn night, costume class), year end finals in Children's and Adult Jumpers and WIHS Equitation World Cup Qualifier FEI Grand Prix, charity auction with items ranging from lessons with top riders to trips to exotic locales.
Why you wouldn't go: Nightmarish logistics that include potential 3am scheduled practice-times and laughably small schooling areas. You may be tempted to part with a ton of money at the charity auction.

NATIONAL HORSE SHOW

When: First week of November

Where: Currently Alltech Arena at the Kentucky Horse Park, previously in Madison Square Garden in NYC among countless other venues

What: One week show that culminates the indoor circuit.

Why you would go: Maclay Finals, U25 Championships, another show that bills itself as the oldest and most prestigious ever.

Why you wouldn't go: You might think you're competing in a rodeo in Alltech Arena. By this point in the circuit you are probably ready for indoors to be over. You dislike the color orange.

CHAPTER TWENTY-ONE

WEF Pre-Circuit

Ice Ice Baby

There exists a short show interregnum between the culmination of indoors in early November and the start of WEF in early January. Most sane riders take a winter break from shoveling money into the coal furnace that is showing. Instead of showing, these riders participate in training practices such as "No-Stirrup November" which is riding without the devices attached to the saddle for the riders' feet. I am told this is the best way to obtain a stronger lower leg position, which encourages good form and the ability to stay with the horse's motions. I think it's more like a weighted bat, designed to make it feel easier after you go back to using stirrups. This is usually a junior or amateur practice—if a professional told me they were dying because of No-Stirrup November, I would be profoundly worried about them. Much like running a half-marathon or following a new diet, No-Stirrup November doesn't seem to work if your entire social media following isn't aware you are doing it.

For quite a few riders, especially professionals, going home after the indoor circuit for a break means going to Wellington, where they have established the closest thing to a permanent home due to its extended and required show schedule. Sensing this opportunity, the showgrounds is also home to a group of Pre-Circuit shows during November and December, for riders who can't take a break or wait to start the grind of WEF. They are mostly smaller shows, though there is an FEI sanctioned show the first weekend after Thanksgiving cutely called "Holiday & Horses." These other shows unabashedly go on during Thanksgiving, Christmas and New Year's, proving the nonchalance some professional equestrians have towards holidays.

The Pre-Circuit exudes a strange, almost calm-before-the-storm atmosphere. Everyone is getting used to the tropical Florida climate, setting up and moving into barns and most importantly, buying and selling horses. The Pre-Circuit is a busy time for the sale of horses. Owners and riders need to line up horses to compete at circuit, and there occurs a large concentration of available buyers and sellers for the first time since WEF ended in April. My girlfriend has a particular affinity for watching other people's horse trials, which I suppose could be construed as entertaining if you had some idea what was going on. A rider, usually of average to minimal talent, tries out a horse for the first time, attempting to put it through the normal training motions. This could lead to some amusing moments, but I have never looked up from my phone long enough during a trial to witness them.

I was flabbergasted when we returned to Florida after a long fall in Tryon only to be greeted by even more shows. "Can't they take a break? Don't they have enough meaningless ribbons?" I whined. Alas, there are always young horses to train, sales horses to show off and clients from which to get show fees. I got my first WEF-like experience during Holiday and Horses, where they hold a similar Saturday Night Lights event, albeit with a holiday flair that would not be welcome in January. WEF partnered with the town of Wellington to host the town's Christmas celebration, so there were big crowds, lots of strange food vendors and even fake snow. It was a bit incongruous with the 75-degree weather and especially gross when I jokingly stuck my tongue out and realized it was mostly comprised of soap. A winter wonderland indeed.

The most exciting event of the night wasn't the Grand Prix but the musical performer afterwards—the one, the only, '90s megastar Rob Van Winkle, aka Vanilla Ice. You see, Mr. Ice has been a Wellington resident for over a decade and it is the setting for his DIY network reality show, *The Vanilla Ice Project*, where I assume he flips houses in between stopping, collaborating and listening. If you already knew this information before you read it and aren't his neighbor or something, then you may need to re-evaluate some choices you've made in your life. I was so flummoxed by the randomness of his appearance that I resorted to more research online, where I learned that he had been a resident of Wellington for some time. He was even named Wellington's citizen of the year in 2014, before having some legal trouble in 2015.[78] So, that's what Vanilla Ice is up to now if you were interested. At the Holiday and Horses show he came out to a couple hundred people who remained after the competition

---

[78] He ended up accepting a community service plea deal, taking the opportunity to tweet out: "Anything less than the best is a felony. Hee hee."

on the side of the arena where a small stage was set. He mercifully began with Ice Ice Baby. As he launched into the first chorus, the heavens opened and it began pouring rain. It suddenly became an unintentional comedy show, as he kept plowing through the song as half the crowd continued in the rain and the other ran in all directions seeking refuge. As is the custom in Florida, the rain subsided shortly after the song ended, just in time for him to play very loud rap/dance music as the fake snow machine fired up. He invited a bunch of kids on stage and they all danced as he sung some terrible songs I had never heard. I left thinking that this had to be the weirdest thing I had seen at a horse show.

CHAPTER TWENTY-TWO

Miami

Bays, Blues and Butts

It was truly paradise for a Horse Show Boyfriend. Instead of sitting at the Walnut ring in the rain watching endless Pony conformation classes, my feet were in the sand, steps away from South Beach's breathtakingly blue water. I was next to females and males in barely-there bathing suits watching top-level international show jumping in pristine early-April weather. It is undoubtedly a positive thing that I experienced the Global Champions Tour Miami Horse Show in its 2nd year, at the end of my travels in 2016. Had I attended in April 2015 shortly before journeying to horse shows around the eastern US, it would have completely ruined anything positive these shows would have had to offer as I sulked about the lack of warm beach and ocean to stick my feet in between classes.

To put it mildly, there was nothing like Miami. It was the only stop in the United States of the 2016 season of the Global Champions Tour, a sort of upper echelon grouping of horse shows in which most of the top riders compete during the year in glitzy places such as Monaco, Paris, Doha and

Shanghai. Many times they plop their temporary showgrounds directly onto scenic vistas such as South Beach, majestic castles, or even the lawn in front of the Eiffel Tower. Most of the top international (European) talent exclusively shows in it, and Miami would be one of the few times one could see some of the world's top riders on American soil. Some top American riders spend most of the season on the tour as well, but the majority of them tend to stay in North America and support their home shows. Virtually all decamp for Wellington during the Global Champions Tour offseason in the winter. My girlfriend was particularly excited to experience in person the hunky Scott Brash, a Brit who won the team Olympic gold in 2012 and at 30 years of age has a reasonable claim as being one of the best in the world. Events like Miami with top riders from Europe we had yet to see was a reminder that there is a vast, strong jumping culture running concurrently to the one here. I don't know if there is some poor European guy going around to all the different shows on the circuit in Europe with his girlfriend and writing about it; but if there is, he is probably too busy enjoying the glamour of shows like Miami to feel the need to write a book about it.

I came in to Miami expecting it to be a cut above in terms of experience due to its status as a Global Champions Tour league, and I was not disappointed. The show ran smoothly the day I was there, and it was even free to attend. They make their money with astronomical entry fees for riders and VIP seating. There are no middle class riders in GCT events—the picture of you jumping with the ocean in the background will cost five figures before you even have to pay the photographer. The fact that anyone can walk up and watch one of the best collections of jumping talent for free is mind-blowing and leads to the amusing dynamic, as foot traffic and beachgoers comprise the majority of the spectators. This results in you feeling positively overdressed in shorts and a T-shirt. I had not previously experienced much South Beach culture outside of Sisqo's "Thong Song" music video. It proved prescient, however, as there were as many mostly bare butts as were bays in the ring. The men were even fond of sporting European-style extremely short shorts as bathing suits. I would have immediately purchased one to change into to feel more at home amongst the crowd, but I couldn't have pulled it off. I have very skinny bird legs. But let's get back to the butts for a minute. This is a horse show where you can stand feet away from the schooling or main rings and see at least one, if not many, ladies' barely-covered bums against the ring wall as horses pass. The juxtaposition is overwhelmingly ironic and hilarious—riders in extremely formal attire of show jackets and breeches, flanked by thongs. While my girlfriend and I were not there to take pictures for once, we couldn't resist capturing this scene and posting it to her twitter account. A girl whose backside was featured in one of the pictures turned out to be a horse person and fan of my girlfriend's blog. She immediately and cheerfully identified herself in a response on Twitter solely by her mostly exposed derriere. Only at a horse show in Miami can you make friends this way.

I could certainly go on about how fortunate it was to have a constant stream of people of the opposite sex in skimpy swimwear to observe when the action in the ring gets boring, but I should probably describe the show before I run out of ways to describe how hilarious and insane mostly naked spectating at a horse show is. I mentioned it before, but the scenery at this show was breathtaking. You can't watch the show without taking in the bright, inviting Caribbean blues of the ocean looming just steps away. On the other side stand large, fancy hotels with untold numbers of rappers inside, cobbling together their next mixtapes between clubbing sessions.

The show consists of one ring with an attached schooling ring, and has varying levels of jumper competition through the weekend. There were no hunters, equitation classes or ponies, though sometimes it felt like there were because of the boring courses. The day I attended, there were lower amateur classes in the ring before the main 5* Grand Prix. It was only a week after seeing my first 5* Grand Prix in person at WEF, which was stunning in terms of jump size and difficulty. This competition is the most difficult outside of major international competitions like the World Cup Finals or the Olympics. Since it was an event in a specialty location, the surroundings took precedence over an intricate course for the riders. They only had a limited amount of space to work with on the shore of South Beach. I had experienced this before at Central Park, which had to work within the oblong confines of an ice skating rink. Central Park certainly felt tight, but more in a way that some horses had trouble with the course than in the course design. It was also only a 3* event, so it required less difficult additions. Miami's course, especially the scaled down version in the smaller classes, was especially bland. As the competition progressed, the ins and outs made it feel more like a hunter course than a compelling jumper course, asking demanding and unique questions of the rider. I can't fault them too much for this, as it is a necessary concession for the location, but it was a little disappointing to have probably the best competition I will see for some time be in a condensed area.

As my girlfriend and I camped out in the afternoon sun at our primo spot in the bleachers, we chatted up two girls behind us who had flown in from New York just for the event. After our travels, I appreciated their dedication to horse show spectating. One of them was originally from Australia, so when I asked who they were pulling for, she cheerfully replied Edwina Tops-Alexander, the only Australian in the field. I hadn't heard of her before since she only comes to the US on the Global Champions Tour (she won the circuit championship in 2011 and 2012) or for World Cup Finals. My girlfriend and I were going through a big McLain Ward phase after watching him dominate WEF, so we were rooting for him and his superstar mare, HH Azur. As the competition dragged on in the afternoon sun, we soon realized that these GCT Grand Prix events had an excruciating addition—a second round before the jump off. So riders come in and jump, then the top 14 advance to the second round, regardless of faults or time. From this, those that go clear in a slightly shortened course will advance to the normal short course jump off. This was wholly unnecessary and turned it into a 3+ hour marathon of uninteresting action in a tight ring. Once the jump-off mercifully arrived, two Americans were left in the final six: McLain and Georgina Bloomberg. McLain predictably but sensationally took the lead with a blisteringly fast round aboard HH Azur and had the win sealed up. But, last to go, Edwina Tops-Alexander bested his time by over a second to take the win. Our Australian friend behind us went nuts.

The events like Miami, Central Park and New Albany will always be able to do things that the WEFs and Tryons cannot, as they have the luxury of holding a horse show in a location for a very brief period of time for a small number of people. It's interesting to see what some of the shows do with that advantage, as it allows each show to highlight their main focus. Miami is a bit less specialty because there are many other events like it under the larger Global Champions Tour umbrella, but this show seemed to be all about the glitz and backdrop. The riding experience took a backseat to the view, and amateur riders were willing to put up with any inconvenience and cost to get the shot of their precious equine nugget jumping on the beach. I would just photoshop myself jumping in the scene and save the tens of thousands of dollars. It was impressive and inclusive that anyone who wandered by could take in the high level show jumping for free. Some would likely leave thinking this was a sport for the very-rich a la yacht racing and not worthy of any second glance. If there is a have-mores of the jumping world, Miami and the GCT was their show, a far cry from the already elevated A-circuit scene. The diverging paths of those riding there illustrated this, as the Americans enjoying their token GCT show would head back to the east coast A-circuit for the summer while the other GCT jet-setters would be off to Mexico City the next week, then to a quick layover in Antwerp before heading to Shanghai. It must be nice, but at least I got to take in this horse show with my feet in the ocean.

EPILOGUE

I am sitting out at a ring in Wellington. It's 7:45am on a Sunday, and I am holding a camera. My girlfriend will come out shortly riding her horse. Her trainer will come soon after to give her a lesson, which I will be filming. Later I will be told that I have gotten too artsy and close up with my shots and that she needs them wider to get the full picture of what she was doing right or wrong. Apparently jumping lessons are not the time to channel your inner Godard. This is just one of many new scenes I find myself in as I transition to the more normal roles of a horse show boyfriend.

After our barnstorming horse show tour, my girlfriend accepted a job in marketing for the show management company for WEF, Tryon, Central Park and Colorado. We now spend the majority of our time in Wellington during the winter and Tryon during the summer, becoming extremely young snowbirds. In addition, I have actually become a real horse show boyfriend, as my girlfriend has started to ride regularly and show. This was a very welcome change, as it was not easy for her to be immersed in something she loved so much without being able to ride and show. It has drastically altered my horse show experience as well, as I have graduated from passive, purposeless spectator to groom, cameraman, gopher, therapist and much more. While I could help take pictures at a show, I am of much less use with most of these new tasks. The last time she showed I actually had to hold her horse when she walked the course, which was a terrifying amount of responsibility. I tried to pretend like I knew what I was doing so her mare wouldn't sense my fear and uncertainty as I led her over to the shade tree at WEF near Ring 9. The smattering of grooms there looked at me quizzically as what seemed like an eternity passed. Eventually I had to start walking her horse around in circles, as she was on to me and I needed to keep her busy so she wouldn't misbehave. She returned and I managed to survive the incident without my foot getting stepped on.

Being a real horse show boyfriend has transformed my activity from covering these shows to more local concerns of actually being in a relationship with someone who regularly rides and competes. Instead of being a passive observer of this crazy ecosystem, I am now confronted with the realities of the costs, time and commitment involved in being attached to someone interested in jumping horses. It makes my hobbies of video games, photography and swimming seem quaint by comparison. Before, I was attending these shows out of sheer curiosity, the desire to photograph them and help my girlfriend with her blog and then her job. Now my presence is mandatory and purely as a spectator and supporter of a rider in the ring. While I have not yet experienced the horror of money from my bank account going to the many costs involved in riding and showing, this is likely an unavoidable future. Some less experienced horse show boyfriends approach this from the perspective of "I want to build you a barn and see you ride in a Grand Prix one day!" My mindset is more "instead of paying show fees, let's just sneak on to the show grounds after they are done and I'll set a course and time you." But as our relationship continues, we will have to make cost-prohibitive decisions how much she is able to ride and show. These will be difficult because of her love of riding and the sport. If this book becomes a New York Times bestseller, then maybe those decisions will be easier, but I probably have a better chance of waking up tomorrow with McLain's equitation. I wish the sport was less burdensome financially. Aspects of it certainly seem overpriced, but the costs involved in owning and caring for a complicated animal can only be reduced so much.

In one of the more sobering moments attempting to discuss horses with show-people, I innocently asked a wealthy owner (even by horse standards) what she liked about horses. She responded, "Nothing. Liking them is a kind of sickness." It immediately made sense to me after witnessing firsthand the amount of money and energy put into the sport over the last two years. There is no half-assing it with horses—they require care and training daily and take a grip on the lives of people involved with them. Riders do it because it's what they love, but there is always a large price to pay even if you have infinite capital to support it. The metaphor of liking horses as a disease hits even closer after confronting the inevitable financial strain supporting the hobby causes. But, having traveled to all these different shows in support of my girlfriend's passion, it seems I too now have a cold coming on.

ACKNOWLEDGEMENTS AND MORE

It goes without saying this book would not be possible without my girlfriend, Meg Banks. Meg, thank you for dragging me along on your horse show journey, and I deeply apologize for all the sidelong glances I gave you that indicated I was ready to leave the show. Thank you for educating me about show jumping and including me in your hobby. I am very proud of all you have accomplished in this sport and can't wait to see what you will do next. Just, please, don't make me go to Pony Finals again.

I had quite a lot of help in the creation of this book. I owe a great deal of thanks to the entire team at Mad Season, LLC for giving me the barn-life experience and especially to its owners, Alex Granato and Josh Dolan. Alex and Josh were very patient with me as I wasted countless dinners extracting horse show information from them. This book and my understanding of the sport would not be what it is without their input. They are two of the best horse show friends I could have asked for, and I feel very fortunate that we encountered them on our journey.

Major thanks are in order to Liza Goodlett for schooling me on college equestrian and all of its intricacies. Thanks to her, I now check the scores of college equestrian more than college basketball. I also owe thanks to all the other horse show people we met going from show to show, especially two riders and their moms that we met early on: Mary Elizabeth Cordia and her mom, Liz, and Grace Howard and her mom Kimberly. Thanks to all those who facilitated our attendance at some of these shows and events, especially Lisa Hinson at New Albany and Kathleen Fallon at Breyerfest.

This book was a mess before I turned it over to a dream team of editors to tear apart. My hall parent at boarding school turned adult friend James Pharr was instrumental in guiding me into making this book a (hopefully) interesting and fun read. My father, Frank Bell, put in numerous helpful edits, all while on a tight schedule at work. This book would be littered with misused colons, gratuitous adverbs and unnecessarily snarky comments were it not for him. My grandmother, Jane Hedrick and Meg's mother, Valerie Brown also lent their expert proofreading skills. Thanks to the rest of my family, including my mother Laura Lu and grandfather Bob for being very supportive of my crazy endeavors.

I owe thanks to two groups of people who made the foundation of this book possible as well. The first is the group of English and writing teachers that had the misfortune of attempting to instill knowledge on me. Something must have rubbed off despite all evidence to the contrary at the time. Thank you, Ms. Hoekstra, Ms. Wilson, Mr. Prickett, Mr. Bonner, Ms. Whitworth, Mr. Wilson and Dr. Singerman. And a deep thank you to Ms. Reid for making sure I graduated. The second group I should acknowledge are the friends that for better or worse helped developed the sense of humor needed to crack jokes about hunters. Thank you Austin Stevens, Craig Stewart, Joey Tabler and Grant Clark. I fully understand if none of you read this.

I owe a special thank you to the crazy group of mysterious people on eq anon island on Twitter for embracing my Horse Show Boyfriend account in its nascent stages. I want to also thank all the fantastic riders that put on a show in the ring during my travels and helped me fall in love with the sport. Finally, I want to thank my college buddy Steph Curry and the

Golden State Warriors for winning the NBA championship while I was traveling around to all these shows. It was amazing, and I am ready for another one.

In addition, I didn't want to put color pages with tiny pictures in the book, so, if you go to my website at www.horseshowboyfriend.com, I've posted a number of pictures of me at the various shows and the scenes I describe in the book.

42864929R00126

Made in the USA
Middletown, DE
24 April 2017